STEWART WHITE RETURNS:

"'Part of the pursuit of spiritual growth and awareness is learning each step thoroughly. It's unfortunate that so many modern people want instant awareness. There is no such thing."

—Stewart White

"'Everyone of you has lived ten thousand times ten thousand lifetimes in the physical plane. And you will probably live that many more. Those who go around playing the reincarnation game, saying that they *know* this is going to be their last incarnation and that they have completed their evolution, are very foolish."

—Stephen

"'I don't want the flying saucer enthusiasts to get all excited over this, but there are intelligences living on other planets, and it is meant for man to travel. Man has already traveled off this planet eons ago, but you have all forgotten how to do it—intentionally."

—Stewart White

"'That's what Satan is—the one who teaches people to be nothing, to be no-thing, a naught, a zero, a vegetable. Now, a real turnip is a beautiful thing, but a human who is trying to be a turnip is something gross. The whole proposition is repugnant."

—Joan

"'In a very real sense, a human being is like a 'skin' between two universes. The inward universe is every bit as vast and as real as the outward one."

—Stewart White

FROM HEAVEN TO EARTH:

STEWART WHITE RETURNS

BY ROBERT R. LEICHTMAN, M.D.
THROUGH THE MEDIUMSHIP
OF D. KENDRICK JOHNSON

The Twelfth In A Series

ARIEL PRESS
THE PUBLISHING HOUSE OF LIGHT
COLUMBUS, OHIO

Second Printing

This book is made possible by gifts
to the Publications Fund of Light.

STEWART WHITE RETURNS

ISBN 0-89804-062-0

A BRIEF INTRODUCTION

for the benefit of readers who are becoming acquainted with our series, From Heaven to Earth, *for the first time*

Stewart White Returns is the twelfth in a landmark series of books written by Dr. Robert R. Leichtman. Each book in this series is the transcript of a conversation between Dr. Leichtman and the spirit of a well-known genius or psychic, conducted through the mediumship of David Kendrick Johnson. The interviews, which were mostly conducted in 1973, grew out of an idea of Dr. Leichtman's to write a collection of biographical sketches which would rekindle public interest in the exploration and investigation of the human mind and psychic potential.

As Dr. Leichtman began composing a list of the people he might wish to write about—people such as White, William Shakespeare, Edgar Cayce, C.W. Leadbeater, Eileen Garrett, Nikola Tesla, Thomas Jefferson, and Arthur Ford—it occurred to him that all of them had left the physical plane. Not only that, but they were also all people with whom he had communicated through direct clairaudience at one time or another. So, rather than just write biographical sketches of them, he reasoned, why not speak to them *directly*—through a medium—and let them talk about their lives, experiences, inspirations, and current thoughts *in their own words!*

The choice of a medium was an easy one. Dr. Leichtman immediately thought of his good friend, David Kendrick Johnson. Dr. Leichtman knew that Mr. Johnson had been "entertaining" Cayce, Jung, Madame Blavatsky, and many of the others on his list for quite some time already. And he respected David's talent as a medium to work compatibly with creative and innovative spirits. A first-rate artist in his own right, David has the understanding and competence which make it possible for other creative geniuses to speak through him, mediumistically. So Dr. Leichtman broached the idea. Mr. Johnson responded enthusiastically.

By the time they began the series of interviews, Dr. Leichtman and Mr. Johnson had drawn up a rather impressive list of people to converse with—heavily weighted toward those who had been gifted with unusual inspiration and vision while alive in the physical body. They decided, for example, to contact such outstanding mediums and pioneers in the exploration of life after death as Ford, Cayce, Garrett, and White. Also making the list were a number of mysterious, "occult" personages: Cheiro, the actor-turned-palmist who gained much fame in Europe with his amazing predictions around the turn of the century; the controversial Madame Blavatsky, who helped found the Theosophical Society and who claimed to be in contact with superhuman "Masters"; and Bishop

Leadbeater, the clergyman who became a clairvoyant and author of many books on the invisible dimensions of life. Rounding out the list were a number of geniuses who obviously had led inspired lives while being less overtly psychic: William Shakespeare; the psychologists Carl Jung and Sigmund Freud; Thomas Jefferson; Nikola Tesla, the electrical genius; and Sir Oliver Lodge, the British physicist, educator, and early psychic investigator.

As the series' title, *From Heaven to Earth*, suggests, the purpose of this project is to acquaint readers with the current thinking of these outstanding individuals, even though they have left their physical bodies and now work on the inner dimensions of reality. Many new ideas about psychology, psychic phenomena, science, literature, human civilization, and the future of mankind are set forth in these conversations—as well as plenty of good humor.

It is not the intent of this series to document the existence of life after death—or the effectiveness of mediumship in contacting the spirits of those who have left their physical bodies. Nor is it necessary, for these matters have been scientifically proven many times over in other writings—indeed, in many of the books written by the people interviewed in this series. The doubting reader will find ample proofs in the works of Sir Oliver Lodge, Stewart Edward White, Eileen Garrett, Madame Blavatsky, C.W. Leadbeater, Arthur Ford—and countless others.

Instead, the interviews in *From Heaven to Earth* are offered as a way of demonstrating that we need not be content with just an echo of great geniuses who have lived and died; their voices can literally be heard again.

Their spirits and ideas can actually return to earth. Heaven is not some faraway place inaccessible to mortals. It can easily be contacted by competent psychics and mediums who have correctly trained themselves—as have Dr. Leichtman and Mr. Johnson. And such contact can produce insights and new ideas of great importance.

A more complete introduction to this series is contained in the first book, Edgar Cayce Returns. *In it, the nature of the mediumistic trance, the origins of this specific project, and the value of creative genius are discussed in detail. For information on ordering this first volume in the series, please see page 94 in this volume.*

—Carl Japikse
ARIEL PRESS

STEWART WHITE RETURNS

The story of Steward Edward White is a tale of a pioneer's adventure into new and uncharted realms—not the Western frontier of the American pioneer, which was one of the favorite themes of Stewart's fiction, but the frontier of the mind and the subtle realms of creation. His tale is not unique: many mediums and clairvoyants have explored this frontier. But most of them do so without really trying to comprehend what they are exploring, or map out what they discover in any coherent way that can help others find their way, too. Therein lies a great problem, producing more superstitions and theories about the mind and the inner planes than actual facts. Stewart White, however, is an important exception to the usual rule. He ignored the common practices of pandering to the hopes and expectations of those who merely want to communicate with the spirits of the dead, and focused instead on *charting consciousness itself*.

Actually, the story of Stewart White is the story of more than Stewart alone. It is also the story of his wife Betty and their close friends Darby and Joan. Together, they mounted one of the most impressive expeditions into the inner planes recorded in occult history. Joan and Betty were the mediums; Darby and Stewart, the questioners, trying to understand the nature of the inner worlds their wives were exploring. And, it is the story of a number of spirits, too, most notably Stephen.

It was Stephen who first contacted Darby and Joan shortly after his death as a soldier in World War I. Prior to that, Darby and Joan had had no contact with the world of the occult, but Stephen helped them develop their talents and led them, step-by-step, on an exploration of the subconscious, mediumship, the nature of consciousness, the subtle realms, and the principles of rebirth. Out of these experiences, Darby and Joan wrote the book, *Our Unseen Guest*, which became one of the classics of mediumistic literature.

Shortly afterward, Betty and Stewart White also began their investigation of the inner worlds, without, at that time, knowing Darby and Joan. After a certain amount of trial and error, they discovered that Betty was mediumistic. At about that time, Stewart discovered *Our Unseen Guest* and was greatly benefited by it. Eventually, the two couples met each other and became good friends.

Even though Stewart was a popular author of western fiction—he wrote more than forty novels during his lifetime—it was fifteen years before he published the adventures he and Betty had shared on the inner planes. That story was told in *The Betty Book*, one of the most widely-read books on the occult today. This was followed a few years later by *Across the Unknown.* These two books chronicled Betty's development as a medium and shared the more important insights the Whites had gained.

In early 1939, Betty died, thus setting the stage for new discovery. For, now that she was a spirit herself, she found that her new perspective made her an even better investigator than when she had acted as medium. So, with Joan serving as medium, Betty proceeded to lead Darby and Stewart through a lengthy "divulgence" about the nature of the inner planes, which she labeled "the unobstructed universe." The earth plane, she said, was the obstructed universe. To understand the nature of spirit, one must start thinking in unobstructed terms.

It was not easy for Stewart and Darby to understand all the points Betty was trying to convey, but they kept asking questions until their confusion was cleared up. After more than forty carefully-recorded sessions, Stewart sat down at the typewriter and wrote out one of the most precise and comprehensive descriptions of the inner planes which has yet been published. He titled it, appropriately, *The Unobstructed Universe.*

Wisely, Stewart did not just put forth the conclusions the four of them had reached, leaving it to the reader to make sense of them. Instead, he chose to lead the reader on the same journey they had taken—step by hesitant step into the unobstructed universe. The gradual development of the major ideas presented is one of the great virtues of this book. Not only does it help the reader understand very abstruse ideas more readily, but it also gives him important insight into the problems involved in the higher varieties of mediumistic communication.

The art of communicating through mediums can be difficult enough, but when intelligent conversations on complex subjects are attempted, new factors of difficulty emerge. The personality of the medium, for example, can become a limitation. So can the types of questions asked and even the interest of the physical people listening. Fortunately, this was not a problem in the exploration of the unobstructed universe. Rather than sitting like two sacks of potatoes, waiting for Betty and the other spirits to initiate the conversation, Stewart and Darby questioned and requestioned them vigorously, until they had worked out a suitable model for understanding the nature of consciousness.

This, of course, is the only way to have an intelligent communication through a medium. Spirits tend to be very limited if the physical people they are talking with do not hold up their end of the conversation with intelligent questions and comments.

Stewart White wrote a number of other books after *The Unobstructed Universe,* but I believe this one to be his greatest contribution. It is actually a basic introduction to fourth-dimensional thought and reality. In the physical plane, we deal primarily with three dimensions. As we enter the inner worlds, however, we begin working with a fourth dimension. Little is known or written about the fourth dimension; although many clairvoyants and mediums have investigated the inner worlds, their perceptions and reports have been made almost exclusively in three-dimensional terms. Mathematicians and others have speculated and theorized on it, creating complex mathematical models and elaborate schematic drawings. But these models lack the flavor and substance of the real fourth dimension, which is a universe in itself, interpenetrating the three-dimensional universe we are familiar with.

In *The Unobstructed Universe,* Stewart White charts the fourth dimension, without even calling it that, in a very helpful way. He invents new terms—words like orthos, co-existent essence, and pluralistic monism—but they are necessary in order to convey the basic message that time, space, and motion are different in the unobstructed universe of the fourth dimension than they are in the third dimension. To learn to think fourth-dimensionally, we must first comprehend these fundamental differences.

It is not an easy book to read: it is challenging. But it represents an effort which has not been duplicated by any other modern book. It is truly a landmark in the literature of mediumistic communications. For that reason, it is well worth whatever amount of studying is required to master its ideas.

Whenever I read or reread any of the books written by Stewart and Betty, Darby and Joan, I cannot help admiring the way they pursued their work. In a field filled with uncritical thinkers and undistinguished writers, they skillfully used common sense and intelligent skepticism to focus, challenge, and invoke the ideas and comments brought through the medium. As far as possible, their efforts were free of the preconceived notions, religious dogma, Spiritualistic axioms, or low level hysteria which so commonly mar other journeys into the inner planes. They relied on their own intelligence, not prefabricated superstitions. That is always the best course for anyone seeking an enlightened understanding of the mind and the heaven worlds.

Personally, I believe that one of the best decisions these four people made was to stay away from the usual conventions of mediumship. In the early twentieth century, for example, when Betty and Joan were developing their mediumship, the training of mediums was dominated by Spiritualism. This tended to confine mediumship in rather rigid ways. It also led to the belief that only Spiritualists could properly train a medium—which is nonsense. The true training of mediumship is supervised by the spirits who work with the medium. It is not done on the physical plane.

Indeed, the early books by the Whites and Darby and Joan—especially *Our Unseen Guest* and *The Betty Book*—are very good records of the intelligent unfoldment of mediumship and psychic ability.

One other point that has always impressed me about the Whites is their constant effort to impress upon their readers that we all live in the realm of spirit right now. It is not just spirits who live on the inner planes—physical people do, too. The only difference is that those of us on the physical plane are obstructed in our understanding of our inner existence.

It is not uncommon for psychics and mediums to indicate that our life in the heaven worlds begins at the time of physical death. This is common religious belief as well. But the Whites stressed the fact that facets of our consciousness are alive and well in heaven even now. The key to our growth lies in recognizing this inner activity and trying to focus it in meaningful ways into our daily activities in the obstructed realms.

In the interview that follows, I chat with Stewart, Joan, and Stephen. It is a free-ranging conversation, covering many different topics. We kept Stewart busy talking about the development of mediumship and clarifying certain points made in *The Betty Book* and *The Unobstructed Universe*. Joan followed with some biting comments about those mediums and psychics who practice "mental deadness." When Stephen came in, he held us spellbound with his discussion of creativity and what he termed "the rape of the mind"—a very serious problem in modern society.

Throughout the discussion, we freely used a number of terms coined by the Whites in their books. Rather than attempt to define them all in the course of the text, I have chosen to add them to the glossary at the end of the book. They are all clearly labeled as being terms used by the Whites, and defined as they defined them.

For the interview, Stewart, Joan, and Stephen all speak through the mediumship of my friend, David Kendrick Johnson. I ask most of the questions, but am joined by Paul Winters, who was the medium for Sigmund Freud in *Jung & Freud Return;* David's wife, Colene; and a friend we shall call John Hewitt. The interview was conducted in the summer of 1973.

Leichtman: Where would you like to begin?

White: Betty asked me to give you apologies today, as she is busy with someone else, dictating. She may be able to come in for awhile later on this evening, but she's busy working on a book.

Leichtman: I see. Well, let me start with a question about the work you and Betty and Darby and Joan did during your lifetimes. I presume this was a carefully planned piece of work, designed to demonstrate how psychic abilities operate and can be used for worthwhile investigation into the subtle realms. Is it safe to say this work was planned out before you incarnated?

White: Oh, yes. Anyone involved in projects of this nature has spent a long time, in many incarnations and between them, preparing for his work. The personality is not always aware of the nature of this preparation, of course. But yes, our work was very carefully set up in advance.

Leichtman: I find it unfortunate that so many people tend to think of immortality and karma in such limited terms. It's important for people to realize that there *is* continuity of work and purpose from one life to another.

White: Absolutely. Even the problems physical people sometimes grieve so excessively over are frequently important parts of their continuing work and purpose, if they could only see them in that perspective. If a person could look at the history of his incarnations, there would be certain dominant themes of activity, all leading to an ultimate creative destiny. These themes *are* the continuity.

Leichtman: Well, what kind of themes would these be?

White: Oh lord, all kinds of themes. For most people, the primary theme is their personal growth. But for some, the theme might be the emergence of leadership talents; for others, the appreciation of beauty. One of your themes would be teaching—just as one of ours is mediumship. There would also be a series of what would seem to be discrepancies in that continuity, but they aren't discrepancies at all. They are part of the preparation. For instance, the person developing leadership talents might go many lifetimes without actually being a leader. Instead, he might have a life experience as the victim of a nagging spouse, another in which he's held back by an angry father, and a third in which he's manipulated by a devious business partner. After all, a *real* leader must know how to deal with manipulation, intimidation, and criticism, as well as inspire others.

The work the four of us are doing now is part of the same work we did physically—and was just as carefully planned and prepared for. We feel very fortunate that we are able to continue our work. I know you grit your teeth when the Seth material is mentioned [*Seth Speaks* and other books by Jane Roberts], but you should know that we have contributed our share of help to that project.

Leichtman: Well, I have difficulties with those books because of some inconsistencies and incompleteness in the ideas they present. I appreciate, however, that the transmission of information through a medium is fraught with difficulty. Darby and Joan's book, *Our Unseen Guest,* very brilliantly lays out some of the limitations a medium's or a psychic's subconscious can impose on a spirit, by distorting it or even rejecting it entirely. More people ought to read that book; it's a major contribution to occult literature.

John Hewitt: And you mention "coloring" many times in your books.

White: The subconscious of the medium or psychic coloring ideas and messages, yes.

Leichtman: And you also had the even tougher problem of bringing through elaborate and fundamental concepts of abstract time, space, and motion.

White: That material could only be presented under special conditions. In looking back now, I can see how carefully we prepared for the work of *The Unobstructed Universe.* Joan was a very erudite woman and had done an excellent job of mental housecleaning, as had Betty. We had all been good friends for many years, and had a strong rapport. As a result, after Betty "died," she was able to bring through Joan ideas and concepts that would otherwise be too easily distorted in ordinary mediumship.

I'm going to use the names "Betty" and "Joan," even though they are not their real names. It doesn't really matter, but your readers will be more familiar with the ordinary set of names.

You might talk to David when we break this afternoon; we are giving a slightly different version of trance than he is used to. He's virtually on the other side of the county at the moment.

Hewitt: In reading *The Betty Book,* I noticed that Betty would often describe where her consciousness was and relate it to the subject matter being discussed. Of course, at times the invisibles would correct any misinformation she might come across. Can the same be said of David right now—is he experiencing these same things? Is he aware of your presence and the presence of other spirits working with him? Can he discern them? Where is David's consciousness?

White: Well, David is usually standing in the room during a trance—or something of him is standing in the room. [*Chuckling*] It can be rather startling the first time a medium "turns around" and sees himself standing in the room. But with time, it's something he gets used to.

David is aware that I am here. We met at the start of the trance, and he knows who is here. Usually, he is also aware of other beings in the room, but we have him doing something else today. The best way I can put it is that he is going to school—not in a physical building, but he's being taught something. You might ask him about it when he comes back.

Hewitt: I remember from reading *The Unobstructed Universe* that Betty gave vivid descriptions of how Joan appeared to her—as various emanations of color and pulsation. I know that at the time that work was being done, it was difficult for you to completely comprehend what she was saying. I'm sure you can now. Can you clarify these descriptions for us? What is it like to observe other individualizations of awareness—from where you are now?

White: When I see nonphysical people, they don't have fingers and toes; they are more like pulsating balls of light. It's a little difficult to describe the differences in appearance between a nonphysical and a physical person, as I see them now. At the moment, of course, I am using a physical body, so my view is not the one I usually have. I see you as you appear physically, but as though you were crocheted, because I am seeing your etheric body more than your dense physical form.

Leichtman: What you are saying seems to be a confirmation of the notion that even though we live in the obstructed universe—the physical plane—we also do live in the unobstructed universe—the inner planes.

White: Yes. Too many people forget that even while they are incarnate in a physical body, they are also a spirit.

Now, if I was in my normal state and not using David's body, John would not appear to me visually, in the usual sense. I would "feel" his appearance more than I would "see" it. That's not quite right, but it gives you the idea; it's hard to describe in physical terminology.

Leichtman: You would sense his presence with your nonphysical senses.

White: We can see the physical world, but not in the same way you do, because we don't have physical organs anymore. As a matter of fact, the physical world appears more beautiful to us than it does to you, because we can see all that there is—and then some. You see only in part.

Leichtman: Yes. To use your terms, you are seeing the co-existent essence.

White: Yes.

Hewitt: Is one's spiritual body largely determined by his character?

White: By your character as developed over several lifetimes and several interludes on the other planes. This is the character of the immortal part of you.

Hewitt: I recall a description in *The Betty Book* where Betty observed the spiritual bodies of various entities on the physical plane, and she found that those who indulged in mainly material pursuits had uglier spiritual bodies than those with a more spiritual awareness. And she could distinguish among them; in fact, she said the spiritual body has a kind of fibrous but definitely cellular shape to it. And then she was immediately corrected by several of the invisibles, but I didn't really follow their correction. I was left with the inference that the spiritual body is distinct and largely shaped by the character of the physical, conscious mind.

White: I'll try to answer this question, but it will be difficult. Bear in mind that Betty was sometimes physical, sometimes nonphysical when she was doing the work recorded in *The Betty Book*. And I am not physical, although I am borrowing a physical body at the moment. The use of David's body, although necessary, produces a kind of distortion. Betty experienced the same kinds of distortions, and that's why she had some problems explaining what she saw. She knew what it is like to see a physical person from over here, but she had difficulty in relating the nature of those perceptions to the rest of us. That's why certain corrections had to be made.

In trying to describe the way John appears to me, for example, I could relate my impressions of the body I see around him to the way I remember things being when I was in the physical. Therefore, I have a *sense* of fingers and toes, but I don't really see them. I infer them.

Now, the same principle can be extended to viewing the shape and nature of someone's spiritual body. You don't have to be on the other side to see this body, by the way; it's the type of perception the aura reader is making. Of course, there are many kinds of aura reading, some trivial and some worthwhile. The best kind is where the psychic is actually perceiving the quality and purity of the other person's spiritual body.

It's very unpleasant to "see" elements such as greed and materialism in the spiritual body of people, because you don't see them as much as you interact with them. It's not like you're viewing a photograph which has no impact on you; you are being touched, at least to some degree, by the unpleasant elements themselves. This is true even if you are only picking up the sensation of these elements from a person walking by you on the street. Unfortunately, all too many people have these unpleasant elements in their character.

I would describe the sensation of perceiving these aspects of character as being something like feeling the rough bark of a tree. But it can also be worse than that: many of these very materialistic people literally project psychic tentacles from their solar plexus, which they use to grasp the objects of their greed or lust. It's extremely unpleasant to perceive these tentacles.

Leichtman: That sounds like the equipment of the psychic vampire.

White: Yes, and you know from your own experience that you don't just "see" these people—they come looking for you. They reach out psychically and drain away your energy, which can be very annoying. Now, this is the invisible part of greed and lust; people don't ordinarily see it, but it happens all the time.

Of course, the greed and lust are not always conspicuous. It's the tendency to be very self-centered which leads these people to want to take your energy.

I'm afraid I've gotten somewhat off the question.

Leichtman: The nature of the spiritual body.

White: Actually, it would be difficult for even a good clairvoyant to see my spiritual body—he would tend to see me as having fingers and toes and wearing a suit, because that's the way his "computer" works. The one up here [*pointing to David's head*], under the hair. As a matter of fact, most of us on the inner planes react to each other as though we had something like a physical body, because we remember from our physical lifetimes what it is like to have one. It is easier to relate to one another this way.

Leichtman: In occult terms, what is it you are referring to as the "spiritual body"? It doesn't sound very spiritual to me.

White: I'm using the term rather loosely.

Paul Winters: Is this the "beta body" that's described in *The Betty Book?* Would it help if you distinguished among the spiritual body, the beta body, and the astral body?

White: What I was just talking about was the astral body. That's the body that preserves the unpleasant elements of character. And it's the body that the clairvoyant is perceiving when he reads an aura or "feels" an impression.

Leichtman: I've always thought it's better not to call that the "spiritual body." I'd be more comfortable calling it the "spook body." [*Laughter.*]

White: Oh, that's very good. Of course, now I no longer have an astral body, and that's the reason why I said it would be difficult for even a good clairvoyant to see it. To borrow David's terms, the astral body stays with the spirit until he is ready to leave the "vestibule." [*See glossary.*] In occult terms, I suppose you would say that I am using my mental body. Of course, I am actually using David's *physical* body. [*Laughter.*] It gets very complicated. I'm trying to put it in understandable terms.

Leichtman: Are you also using part of David's astral body?

White: Not quite in the sense I think you mean

that. As long as I am inhabiting David's physical body I am also inhabiting part of his astral body. But he is using an aspect of his own astral body, too. As you know, the astral body can subdivide and be in several places at the same time.

I have to use part of David's astral body because otherwise the physical body would not function.

Leichtman: You also need it, do you not, for the mediumistic connections?

White: And for the memory banks, which are partly in the astral. The description you have been given of the keyboard is all right, I suppose, but it does misrepresent a little bit what we are doing. However, I can't explain it any better.

Leichtman: It does adequately explain some of the limitations involved in receiving information mediumistically.

Well, we haven't quite wrapped up the question about the beta body, the astral body, and the spiritual body. Can you continue on that?

White: What was the question? I don't remember.

Leichtman: How would you relate the terms beta body, alpha body, and spiritual body to the standard occult terms—astral body, mental body, causal body, and so on?

White: The beta body is the mental body. None of the terms corresponds precisely with the astral body. Betty was quite aware of the astral body, but when she was working from the other side, she found it very cumbersome.

This may be of interest to you: those of us on the mental plane can extrude into the astral plane and

BETTY WHITE

develop an astral counterpart of what we looked like in any given lifetime. To work through David, I have to extrude myself into the astral plane. Part of his astral body and part of my astral extrusion become like two hands holding each other. I'm not using David's and he's not using mine; we are just holding on to each other. David has given up the use of some of his will so that I can will the use of his speech patterns. It's very complicated to explain, but easy to do.

Leichtman: The alpha body is really the physical body, isn't it?

White: Yes.

Leichtman: Was there something distinguishing about the term "spiritual body"? Can you clarify that?

White: It was not meant to describe the body of any one plane. It can be used to refer to any of the inner bodies. Betty used the label, I'm being told, to describe the inner *essence* of a being. The essence is not related to a specific plane, because we live on more than one plane simultaneously.

Most people, of course, are unaware that they live on the finer planes as well as the physical plane. The trained psychic can move back and forth with ease, but this is a skill which has to be developed. The ordinary person doesn't have it, because he has never acclimated himself to the fuller dimensions of reality. Then, when he becomes a citizen of the inner planes, he can have a little difficulty in getting around.

Some of these people remain in the vestibule quite awhile. They almost have to be taught how to walk again, because the adjustment is so difficult. But for physical people who have an awareness of the inner planes, or who prepare themselves for the transition, the period in the vestibule is very short. There is an immediate example here in the room—Colene's grandmother made a very quick adjustment to being on the inner planes, and was even able to attend her own funeral. That may sound a bit morbid to you, but it was important to her. It was just a matter of hours for her to make the adjustment to moving around on the inner planes.

Many people wind up staying somewhere on the high astral between incarnations, because it is more comfortable or familiar for them than the beta body. There is more visual sensation and they seem to need these reference points. Otherwise, they are lost. But those people who are expanding their understanding of life will find there is no problem getting acclimated to the mental plane as well as to the astral.

Leichtman: We are talking about the actual "awareness mechanism," to use one of your terms. How far can an incarnate person go in improving his use of the awareness mechanism and, to use another of your terms, the quantity of his consciousness?

White: There is much that can be done. If the person is a medium and is pursuing his contacts intelligently, he will become very familiar with the inner planes. Right now, for example, David is being given a lesson which is helping familiarize him with one of the inner planes. Betty benefited in this way, too, while she was still in the physical.

Leichtman: But not everyone is a medium.

White: Anyone who learns to work in a true meditative state gradually finds he is able to move around on the inner planes quite easily—especially if he is responsive to help from discarnate friends.

Leichtman: Can these lessons be learned during the periods when the physical body is asleep, too?

White: Sure, and in experiments with astral travel, too. But not everyone who falls asleep or astral travels learns much about the inner planes. If they are still materialistically oriented, their experiences will still be earthbound. Just being able to disconnect from the physical body is not a guarantee that the awareness mechanism is being developed.

Some people who experiment with astral travel are just dilettantes, and frightening things can happen. Some people get out and travel off to Mars or somewhere and forget where they left the body. They get lost. This seldom happens more than once, but it can be rather frightening. These people need to pursue their experiments with a little more circumspection. They should start with simple maneuvers, like moving across the room, until they become comfortable with what's occurring.

Leichtman: Where is the "awareness mechanism" located, and what exactly is it?

White: The awareness mechanism is the equivalent of the five, six, and seven senses you are familiar with in the physical environment. It is seated in the immortal germ, if I might put it that way.

Leichtman: That's not to be confused with the immortal virus, is it? [*Laughter.*]

White: No, I'm using the word "germ" in the sense of the seed of consciousness.

When a person is entering into a physical lifetime, he extrudes some of this awareness mechanism into physical form: the eyes, hearing, and other sensory devices. The problem of contacting the awareness mechanism while in physical life is that most people begin by confusing these physical extrusions for the awareness mechanism itself.

Leichtman: It can't be found by listening to the body or the emotions?

White: No. You have to go into a reflective or meditative state to contact it.

Leichtman: Would speculation, meditation, or reflection on the concepts of orthic space, time, and motion help awaken our understanding of this awareness mechanism?

White: Definitely. [*Drily*] It is safe to say that the awareness mechanism can be contacted and known more readily through thinking abstractly in the higher reaches of thought than it can through the thought processes of the average suburban housewife. Intelligent thought, after all, is one of the principal ways of activating the beta body and becoming focused on the mental plane.

Leichtman: What else can you tell us about removing some of the limitations of the obstructed consciousness while we are incarnate?

White: I don't think I can nutshell that very well.

Leichtman: I wasn't looking for a quick answer.

White: Well, it's helpful to become aware of the mechanics of the mind. There are many compartments of the mind that the average person is not familiar with. He is blind to them, and so they seem obstructed to him. So it's important to go through your mental attic and find out what's there, how it got there, and what it's to be used for. This is the great benefit of the mental housecleaning techniques you teach, although there are many other ways people discover the mechanics of their mind. Some do it on their own, some are helped by psychiatrists. Whatever impulse is the starting point, if the search is pursued seriously, it will eventually lead you to the pure awareness mechanism.

You have to develop a methodology of the mind: how it works, what's in there, how it got there, what has to be cleansed, and how best to use it.

Leichtman: And what ought to be there?

White: Oh, absolutely—what's missing but ought to be there is often more important than what's there but shouldn't be. [*Laughter.*] People ought to be more curious—not so much about what's gone wrong, but what the meaning of the events of their life is. They should ask themselves: what talent would help me? What strength would help me? What better understanding would help me? And then they ought to get busy and develop those talents, strengths, and understandings.

Leichtman: You mean "sitting for development" and meditating on bubbles doesn't do it?

White: No. Something that is not often enough remembered is that both Betty and Joan went through a great deal of examining their own mental methodology, and expanding their understanding, to be sure they were in control of the mediumistic process—and to be sure that something valuable would come through, without a lot of distortion and coloration. Both of them trained for their work in much the same way that an athlete trains—not by doing physical exercises, of course, but by exercising their awareness. Step by step, they reviewed the material that came through, refined their perceptions, and developed their skills, until they arrived at the point where the ideas which came through were pure, and not distorted or gibberish or childish.

Leichtman: Yes, *Our Unseen Guest* brings that out quite elaborately.

White: It's discussed there, and I tried to touch on it in *The Betty Book,* but there is still more work involved than someone reading those books for the first time, without any experience of his own, would realize. It really is work! It requires a thorough search of the mind—and I mean searching in *all* dimensions of the mind, including our superconscious wisdom and talent. You have to get to know yourself *really well.*

Hewitt: In *The Betty Book,* you list—as one of the preliminary steps toward reaching greater spiritual awareness—lifting the thoughts beyond the mundane and normal chatter of consciousness. I got a little disturbed, however, because you also cautioned against straining or consciously reaching for definite things. This would apparently lead to blind alleys in which we would remain. This seems to be a paradox: here we are told to lift our thoughts, but we can't do it consciously or strain for an objective. Would you discuss that?

White: It seems to be a paradox because it is not a complete idea. Early in the game, people would settle for objectives which weren't noble enough.

Leichtman: And concepts that are too concrete?

White: Also too petty. Straining makes it difficult, for example, to receive any help from friends on the inner planes. You don't do it all by yourself. By straining and holding too tightly to what you believe is necessary, you can only progress as far as your limited ideas can take you. By contrast, if you are flexible and openminded as you lift your thoughts and sights, it is easier to receive help, accurately observe the events and ideas you encounter, and attain a better perspective on what you are doing. If your attempt is too deliberate or concrete, you're not likely to make much headway.

I suppose that sounds a bit confusing.

Leichtman: No, it's clear. If you set a specific goal and limit yourself to that goal, that will be all you will get. You can't grow in the process. In order for consciousness to grow, you should constantly reevaluate what you want or expect—and how to get it.

Is it also true that there are many intermediate steps in the pursuit of understanding and awareness about any subject? That seems to be one of the messages of *The Unobstructed Universe*—that you don't receive the understanding of these concepts in a single blinding flash of inspiration. Rather, you begin with a relatively concrete notion, expand on it, gradually become aware of more abstract implications, and finally arrive at its essence. Is that the way it happens?

White: Yes, one does have to start in kindergarten and work himself up to first grade, if I may borrow an analogy from you. But too many people want to leap in and get to the end of the book before they even open it. Part of the pursuit of spiritual growth and awareness is learning each step thoroughly. It's unfortunate that so many modern people want instant awareness. There is no such thing.

Leichtman: You mean that sitting quietly and seeing white light isn't enough?

White: It's not enough!

Leichtman: Darn! [*Laughter.*]

White: And besides, the real white light isn't "seen" anyway. That's a very common mistake people make. They see a little astral light and think to themselves, "Oh, wow, wonderful—I'm enlightened!" [*Laughter.*] Enlightenment is produced by contacts with the soul—not with astral light.

It's a profoundly moving experience, but not the kind of event you would want to cheapen with gushy statements about how wonderful it all was. I don't believe I even talked about it after my first encounter with the real white light. Anyone who genuinely contacts the light of their spirit would respond the same way. The people who gush about white light are either getting it from the Peter Pan department or their own subconscious—one of the two.

Leichtman: You mean there are different shades of white? [*Laughter.*] I refer to the quality, of course.

White: There are different levels of light, sure. The subconscious is perfectly capable of making blinding flashes of white light in your psychic eye, because the psychic eye is part of the subconscious.

There are, as you know, thousands of people who sit in little groups throughout the world. We had them in my lifetime, too. These groups all do some kind of "meditation" together and then compare notes about what happened. Many times people in a group are afraid to admit that nothing happened, so they manufacture something on the spot. When they do, they usually talk about all the white light they saw—that's an easy story to invent and doesn't require much imagination. But if someone has had a truly profound experience, they are likely just to report that it was an intensely personal experience, and let it go at that.

Incidentally, groups that sit for psychic development are largely a waste of time. A group will only take you as far as the dumbest member is able to go. People who could advance quite a long ways are frequently held back by the slower members of these groups.

Leichtman: Are you implying that a pooling of consciousness occurs in these groups?

White: Yes. In any human contact, whether on the physical plane or on the inner planes, there is a pooling of awareness. It's been said that in heaven there is no marriage, because our ordinary contact with each other is more like completely merging into someone else. Instead of having a conversation, it is as though both parties become one for awhile.

Leichtman: A communion of your essences!

White: Yes. Sex, particularly in marriage, is as close as this merging can be approached while in the physical life—except by the enlightened person who has learned to focus his awareness in heaven even while he's alive in a physical body. Of course, the act of sex, as I'm referring to it, has to be surrounded and wrapped up in a good deal of love between both parties. Otherwise, it won't work.

Leichtman: I suppose we could coin some new terms here and refer to this sort of group work as "lateral consciousness," as opposed to "vertical consciousness," which would be the pursuit of one's own essence.

White: I couldn't have put it better myself. [*Laughter.*]

Leichtman: Thank you.

White: Now, I better add this: a group that gets together to learn some basic rules is fine, as long as the leader or teacher knows what he's doing. But to *stay* together for the purpose of developing the awareness mechanism is really useless. One's ultimate development is always done alone, because no two people are going to develop in quite the same way.

Are we running short of tape?

Leichtman: We have another minute or two.

White: You should be very happy to have these devices. I remember the tedium of trying to get everything Betty or Joan was saying written down in a hurry. We could have done more if we had had these mechanical marvels.

Leichtman: Yes, we are free to think and plot our next question, while letting the tape recorder do the listening.

White: It's going to be interesting when someone invents a machine you can put over the medium's head that will let us televise our clairvoyant impressions of heaven.

Leichtman: We'll have to stop here; we're running out of tape. What would you like to talk about when we come back?

White: Well, there's a group here I'm working with; we'll have to see.

Leichtman: All right.

[*There followed a short break while the tapes were changed. Then the conversation was resumed.*]

Leichtman: I want to ask about *The Betty Book* and the other books you wrote in that vein. Do you expect a renaissance of interest in them in the future?

White: Well, they are being printed in less expensive editions now, and of course more people are interested in the occult—and are buying more books on those subjects—than ever before. Yes, I think they will be getting around more than they have.

Maybe one in ten will understand some of it. [*Laughter.*] They are over the heads of some people.

Hewitt: Yes—several people I know have indicated that *The Unobstructed Universe* is too difficult for them.

White: This is one of the reasons why we and some other entities got into the Seth project. We decided the Seth material would lead people back to the other books.

Leichtman: It's always been my experience that unless some strain is put on your mental muscles, you can't grow. After all, you don't build physical muscles by just sweeping the floor—you need more strenuous exercise. The same is true of the mind.

White: True, but given the education most Americans receive nowadays, what usually happens when a person hits a sentence he doesn't understand is that he puts the book aside and forgets it.

Hewitt: That has a lot to do with the sincerity or motives of the person reading. If he's reading the book as part of an intellectual game, or because it's the vogue to dabble in psychic phenomena, then what you say will probably happen. But if he's a serious student, he's not going to let the abstruseness of your books be a barrier.

White: Yes.

Leichtman: I'd like to add this thought. During the break, we were saying that perhaps the Western equivalent of the Zen koan is to try to comprehend something that is very profound, and to stretch yourself to seek out the meaning.

White: That's a good point. In fact, this is why H.P. Blavatsky wrote in such mazes. Her purpose was to lead the reader out of his usual frame of thought into another realm.

We had a passing acquaintance with Blavatsky's work; I think we had a copy of *Isis Unveiled* for awhile, but I don't believe either one of us read it. I am informed almost everyone here is used to the Theosophical set of labels. We were entirely without any kind of group contact, so we were pretty much trying to present what we got as we got it. The very same ideas can be discussed with many different labels. It doesn't really make any difference.

Hewitt: Exactly, it gives freshness to the very same concepts. It presents them in a different way which I found most stimulating.

Leichtman: In fact, it keeps you out of a rut which you might fall into if you got stuck on the level of concrete labels.

Hewitt: In *The Betty Book*, there's a strong advocacy of establishing a working balance between physical and spiritual endeavors. The invisibles indicated that there was at that time a tremendous imbalance in the world, stressing the material or the physical at the expense of the spiritual. I wonder if you see any indication of a redress of this imbalance today.

White: Yes, there is movement away from it. Unfortunately, a lot of people trying to pursue a more spiritual life are getting hold of junk material which just keeps their attention focused physically, but there is a movement away from the purely material life. The encouraging thing at this particular time is there's a growing awareness of the difference between those who are just being lazy and rebellious and those who are withdrawing from the materialistic aspects of society to pursue "the sound of a different drummer."

Leichtman: Well, there are protesters and then there are individualists.

White: I'm talking about the group which is loosely labeled "hippies." Many of them are just playing at being against the material life; they are posing as a way of avoiding responsibility. But there is a small handful who are not just hippies. They are actually succeeding in letting go of such a complete involvement with the material plane.

Of course, this is just one visible example of a much larger movement away from materialism. I do not mean to imply that one has to reject material goods and conventional society to become spiritual; there are many other paths which are far more legitimate for most people. But this is an interesting indication that there is more of a movement away from materialism than there was before.

Leichtman: You make a great distinction between people who are materialistic and concrete in their thought and those who are merely acquisitive of physical possessions or contemptuous of physical possessions.

White: Oh, yes!

Leichtman: Would you say that people who are contemptuous of material possessions and money are just as materialistic as those who—

White: Perhaps more so! They often let their fear

or aversion dominate their lives more completely.

There is nothing wrong with having a mind that can operate concretely—that is, pragmatically—but when concrete, materialistic beliefs rule all thought, then you have a materialist.

Leichtman: That would be concrete thinking about earthbound concepts as opposed to concrete thinking about spiritual concepts.

White: Yes—concrete thinking about concrete! [*Laughter.*]

I would like to preface any further comments with a couple of ideas. You can get so used to dissecting ideas and laying them out so you can take a look at them that it is possible to lose sight of the essence that binds those ideas together. In all the conversations about the inner and the outer planes, it begins to sound like all these planes are stacked one on top of the other, like floors in an apartment building. Of course, that's ridiculous; it's not like that at all. All the planes are interlocking.

Leichtman: Interpenetrating?

White: Interpenetrating, yes. Thank you. At the moment, you are sitting on a chair in the physical plane, but you are also sitting on a chair in the astral plane and the equivalent of a chair in the mental plane, and so on. Even a chair has an existence all the way "up"—not physically, of course, but as the basic idea behind the chair. Incidentally, on the plane where the basic idea of the chair has its existence, it is as concrete as the chair on the physical plane. It exists in the terms of that plane. One could "walk through" the basic idea of that chair, but the idea itself is a reality. How often is it said that thoughts are things? When one lives on the inner planes, it becomes apparent that thoughts really are things.

Leichtman: Yes, as Bishop Leadbeater says, you can actually stub your toes on them.

White [*laughing*]: That's good!

I'm going to borrow another statement from Mr. Leadbeater: matter, as you think of it, is just a very dense kind of idea, a thought in the Mind of God working its way out into the outer planes. I'm not a physicist; I don't have the wherewithal to discuss this myself. I may let someone else come in for a moment and help me out. But matter is on its way to becoming something even more dense in another physical plane, strangely enough. This is not the bottommost plane any more, you know.

Leichtman: You are saying that matter is in evolution, too?

White: Well, not in the way that consciousness evolves, but matter does extend itself through the inner planes into the physical plane.

Leichtman: And the matter or substance would appear on each plane differing in form but not in essence?

White: Yes. The etheric counterpart of the chair you are sitting on, for instance, would look very much like the physical chair, except it would look more like a chair crocheted out of light. The etheric counterpart of anything looks like something which has been carefully crocheted, if you can imagine three-dimensional crocheting.

Leichtman: It's a magnetic gridwork for the dense physical substance, isn't it?

White: Yes. And the astral counterpart of the chair

would be essentially the same, but in addition it would contain your psychological reactions and feelings toward the chair. Your subconscious images of chairs would be included, too. It would have all that worked into it in a way; it would make a rather strange piece of furniture if seen physically. [*Laughter.*]

Leichtman: Are you saying that the astral chair will change, depending on who sits on it—or whether it's vacant?

White: Yes. After all, the astral plane is the place where most of the subconscious exists, and the subconscious colors everything you see and do and think. So all your childhood associations and other memories of chairs would affect the way the chair would look on the astral plane. Your associations would be projected onto the astral chair and become part of it.

The mental chair, then, would appear as something analogous to a plan or design for the physical chair.

Leichtman: Could you sit on it?

White: If you were on the mental plane, you could do the equivalent of sitting on the chair, but you must remember that people on the mental plane have no equipment to sit with, in the conventional sense. [*Laughter.*] On the mental plane, you have a somewhat different shape. I'll give you the beautiful side of it; there's no point talking about the ugly side. Try to imagine what a scintillating intellect would look like if it had a physical presence—not the products of the scintillating intellect, but the scintillating intellect itself. I'm slipping up and looking at you all right now through the mental plane, and you all are very much like big puffs of light. There is a type of jellyfish—the name escapes me at the moment—that looks something like this. It scintillates while it swims. We saw one once in an aquarium, and Betty told me that's what people looked like. At the time, I did not know that. That's not an exact description, but it's as close to something physical that she could point out to me.

Leichtman: Unlike our physical bodies, the mental body would not have dense organs which stay in one position, would it?

White: No.

Leichtman: It's in constant circulation, isn't it?

White: There are organs of a sort, but they are made of mental matter and operate differently than physical organs. You do have what might be called "thought fingers" and "thought toes," but bear in mind that we are talking about the complete mind of a whole being, not just the intellect as it is thought of in the physical plane.

Now, if you get higher than the concrete mental plane and look for the chair again, you would bump into the idea of "chairness." With people, there's even an individualization on the next higher plane, but it's difficult to describe in English. It's a kind of at-oneness. You are still separate identities, but are more in harmony with each other.

Leichtman: More like a cell in the body of mankind?

White: Actually, more like a cell in the body of God. Either way you look at it, from the top side or the bottom side, it's all right.

Leichtman: You mean, then, there is a much greater degree of group awareness or connection with the group of mankind or the body of God?

White: Yes. And going up beyond that is very

difficult, because it is—

Leichtman: Are you talking about the buddhic plane now?

White: If that's a handy label for you, let's use it. Now, the buddhic plane is very difficult to talk about at all, because it is all sights, all sounds, all sensations, all feelings—without any of these things.

Leichtman: It would be the essence of these things, wouldn't it?

White: Describing it is like trying to conceive of how a deaf man can hear music. He hears the music but doesn't have the organs to hear it.

Leichtman: You have direct knowing and direct experience, without the intermediary of sensory impressions?

White: Yes; as a matter of fact, the "sensations" of that level are more closely akin to breathing than to seeing or listening. Things pass through you; you don't assimilate them, but you get an awareness of them as they pass through you and go on. And the sense of separation is even less, because everything is passing through everything else. This is why it is so difficult to talk about it in concrete terms. It is indescribably beautiful, but it cannot be discussed in terms of seeing things or hearing things. You know and are aware—much more powerfully than at the lower levels—but not in the same context that your language is geared to describe.

Leichtman: I suppose you are still yourself, but your appreciation of the dimensions of your total self has expanded to encompass other individuals.

White: It has expanded, but not in a spatial sense. Our words are so inadequate for this kind of discussion—I say "going up in the planes" and you say "expanding," but these terms are figurative. For a physical person—and there are many who have experienced mental and buddhic consciousness during physical lifetimes—you are really going within yourself.

There is a movie that came out a few years ago called *Cosmic Zoom*—David is replaying it for me. There's a little boy in a boat with a dog; the camera backs off and you see the lake, and then the city, and the countryside, and then the planet, and finally the other planets in the solar system, and all the stars. And then the camera zooms back in very quickly and goes inside the skin of the little boy, into the atoms and the molecules, and it looks just like the universe. This is a beautiful analogy for what I'm talking about, but it needs to be taken a step further, because in a very real sense, a human being is a "skin" between two universes. The inward universe is every bit as vast and as real as the outward one. Some day, some philosopher is going to figure out that consciousness is like a Moebius strip—the inward universe and the outward universe are identical. [A Moebius strip, named after the German mathematician A.F. Moebius, is formed by taking a long, thin, rectangular piece of paper, twisting it once, and connecting the ends.] An aware being is something like a Moebius strip; the outside is the inside. Of course, none of you look like that, but that's the way it really is.

Leichtman: Isn't that a sneaky way of saying that the universe is the macrocosm and man is the microcosm, the miniature of the whole?

White: But that leaves out the idea of the inner cosmos and the outer cosmos really being a continuous loop. An individualized awareness—like a human being—is really an inside/outside skin between the two. I am being given some of this to tell you; it's helping me revise some ideas I've had on these subjects in the past. Some of this I simply understand better now that I am a spook, but I'm also taking classes and being taught things I didn't know before.

I must say I'm going to be very lucky when I reincarnate next time. I am going to be able to bring a lot of what I'm being taught now with me and ground it. In a way I am grounding some of it now, but there's nothing like being incarnate. As things stand at the moment, I'm going to be a physicist the next time.

Leichtman: Excellent! A psychic physicist?

White: A psychic physicist!

Leichtman: And a humanitarian, too. Wonderful!

White: And I will get to demonstrate these ideas as they should be. A Mr. Tesla that you know is volunteering to help with that, so it should be very interesting. This is where science is going to have to go to survive—it's going to have to accept the inward/outward universe idea. Many people are beginning to realize that.

Leichtman: I suppose that for growth to occur in any discipline, inspiration is required. The creative effort is always an inspired activity. Do you suppose one could make the study of chemistry or physics a spiritualizing activity?

White: Of course. If it is properly approached, it is an activity of celebrating the Father's handiwork. There is nothing wrong with involvement in the material world—as long as it is approached as a celebration of the Father's handiwork. The world is a very beautiful and interesting place, and the miracles which happen around us every day are great enough that a scientist can easily spend his whole life exploring them.

Leichtman: Isn't it also true that if you really discover the universal laws which govern physical matter, they would also tell you something about your own humanity?

White: Absolutely. The whole field of science is going to be changing rapidly these next few years. The "gentlemen in white upstairs" are going to see to it. The basic occult teachings about the manipulation of astral matter—for instance, to effect a change in the physical plane—are going to be brought down to the level of the direct manipulation of physical matter. There will be a scientist with a rather extended awareness who will be revising current scientific thought on these subjects.

This is how the pyramids were built, you know. Someone knew those laws and how to manipulate physical matter. But most of your current teachings leave out that part.

You know the transporter on *Star Trek?*

Leichtman: Yes.

White: Someone disappears here and then reappears over there in bubbles. That can be done with the mind, and it can have a direct effect on physical objects.

Leichtman: Yes, it would just be a question of creating an etheric vacuum while retaining the pattern, and then recreating it.

White: You make it sound so simple.

Leichtman: It's sort of like deflating a balloon and

then reinflating it elsewhere. [*Facetiously*] I do it all the time. [*Laughter.*]

White: Not really!

Hewitt: How much influence do the "gentlemen in white" have on our affairs?

White: You know who I mean, don't you?

Hewitt: Not really.

White: The "gentlemen in white" are the White Brotherhood. Now, I don't want to make it sound like a men's club.

Leichtman: There are women in it?

White: Of course. After all, almost everyone has been both male and female, one time or another. I don't want to make the White Brotherhood sound like a clockworks, but they are very much concerned and involved with mankind's growth. The nature of their tasks is something akin to keeping the planet earth in orbit. What they do is so influential on the physical plane and on the destiny of man as an organized social group that it is really hard to tell you where they *don't* have an influence. They are not angels, although there are angels who supervise. This is a group of people who are still incarnating and who are very much involved with the physical plane. They are responsible for the physical plane becoming a spiritual plane. Most of you here are involved with the gentlemen in white in one way or another.

Leichtman: They oversee the entire evolution of humanity.

White: Yes.

Winters: There is a lot of talk about the White Brotherhood. Are there other brotherhoods, and if there are, what different functions do they serve?

White: English is limiting again, so I'll put it this way. There are different lodges in the White Brotherhood which sometimes adopt other colors. Some mediums prefer a little more technicolor in their readings, so they come up with purple lodges and the like. There are subgroups that have different assignments. They may announce themselves as the Lavender Hill Mob, for all I know. [*Laughter.*] But they are still part of the White Brotherhood.

Winters: But there is such an overblown idea of what they are.

White: Well, in Eastern studies, the members of the White Brotherhood are called "Bodhisattvas." There are all sorts of names, appellations, and technicolor, but it is all the same thing.

Leichtman: It would be a gross mistake, then, to think that the White Brotherhood is only concerned with theological or religious concepts?

White: Or to assume that the White Brotherhood is going to center itself in Colorado only, or is only concerned with Caucasian man.

Leichtman: Or only centered in San Jose, California?

White: It's ridiculous, isn't it? It's like the silly idea that certain psychics or mediums, once they become spooks, will not appear through mediums themselves—or if they do, they will only appear through a "chosen" medium. You know yourselves this is inaccurate. Many organizations will spread that kind of rumor because they want to control the benefits of that individual's work.

Hewitt: Just as you and other entities are helping Dr. Leichtman and David, are there counterparts who are helping the scientists of today? If so, how directly do they influence scientists? And you might also discuss the space program as having a positive or negative merit.

White: I am going to take the space program first. Man is always going to satisfy his curiosity, and this is healthy. It is meant, you know, for man to travel in the universe. This is intended. However, at the present time there are several influences—and it's not just the White Brotherhood—that are keeping man earthbound. The universal community is waiting for man on earth to grow a bit more.

And yes, there is a universal community of living beings. I don't want the flying saucer enthusiasts to get all excited over this, but there are intelligences living on other planets, and it is meant for man to travel. Man has already traveled off this planet eons ago, but you have all forgotten how to do it—intentionally.

Leichtman: Intentionally?

White: Yes. Scientific thinking is being influenced in slightly misleading directions by beings from another planet so that space flight won't be practical at the present time.

Hewitt: I would think that the space program would be a waste of energies which could be rechanneled for other, greater pursuits on earth.

White: Well, to answer your other question—yes, there are invisibles working with scientists. However, it is virtually impossible for a highly evolved being to help a physical person without his permission. And many scientists are so wrapped up in their statistics and their materialistic view of life that they are seldom able to get an inspiration from a spirit helper. Does that follow?

Hewitt: Yes.

White: There is some activity directed at limiting certain branches of science now, but this work is done by physical agents who know what they are doing and who have direct guidance from their invisible counterparts.

Winters: Would this restriction on our space travel be because of our stage in evolution?

White: Yes! The universal community has "quarantined" the earth for the time being. This is not a punishment; it is just that man on the earth is not ready to join the universal community. And the universal community does not want to be infected at this time.

And all the flying saucers floating around are not from Mars, nor are they hallucinations. There are some that are from other solar systems.

I can also report that the Martians and Venutians are not at war. [*Laughter.*]

Leichtman: And Pluto is not an evil planet? [*More laughter.*]

White: I find it difficult to think that anything the Architect of the universe created is evil.

Leichtman [*facetiously*]: Do you mean the earth is *not* a fallen planet?

White: Where would it fall to? [*Guffawing.*]

Winters: I presume the eventual lessening of this universal control will manifest itself in our ability to get to other planets. We won't all of a sudden be visited by representatives of the universal community and told that mankind is now past the point of censorship, will we?

White: Well, I don't know quite how it's going to be handled, to tell you the honest truth. My own thought is that it would be intelligent for the universal community to make some kind of statement of their presence at that time. Bear in mind that they are very intelligent. I don't know quite what will happen.

Winters: There was a "space message" sent out recently with two pictures in the human form and various symbols. Was that an inspired thing?

White: Apparently it was. I'm having to ask for some help answering that, because the question is a little bit out of my ken. Part of that design was inspired by an extraterrestrial. That little plaque has an additional meaning to the universal community.

Winters: So mankind will see the purpose of that plaque fulfilled?

White: Oh, yes. You may yet see it in your lifetime. Apparently, a lot will depend on what will happen in the scientific community in the next few years.

Are we at a stopping point?

Leichtman: Maybe another five minutes.

White: I'd like to let go of David now; it seems to be an appropriate time.

Leichtman: When we resume after dinner, will we hear from Betty?

White: She will try. Either Betty or Joan will appear. I'm not sure how it will all work out. We have events over here, too, you know.

Hewitt: How about Ann? Is she around?

Leichtman: And Stephen? And the Professor?

Hewitt: Yes. I was really infatuated by Ann.

White: Stephen has incarnated. The others are still here yet. I believe there's going to be a little "chiming in" this evening. We'll see what we can do.

Leichtman: All right. Do stay for din-din, if you can.

White: Yes, we can tune in to the essence of it on the mental plane.

Leichtman: We are having some special liquid you may be interested in. [*Laughter.*]

White: There's a lady here with a rather regal bearing who wants me to tell you that when you eat, we can partake of the mental essence of it. In some ways, it is a case of partaking of your enjoyment of it as much as—

Leichtman: It is the spirit of the spirit into a spirit! [*Laughter.*]

White: And this lady wants me to inform you that when you toast the spirits, she enjoys it very much, and joins in.

Leichtman: Oh, very good.

White: And she's not the only one. We have parties, too, you know. The guest lists would sometimes stagger your imagination. [*Laughter.*]

Leichtman: And I bet you serve super-prana. Well, very good. We'll be back after dinner.

[*There followed a lengthy intermission for wining and dining. When the interviewing resumed, it was not Stewart who returned or Betty, but Joan.*]

Joan: I don't know where to begin, because I didn't listen to the last part.

Leichtman: What would you like to talk about?

Joan: Would you like to speak to Stephen?

DARBY AND JOAN

Leichtman: Whomever, but I'm sure you have something to say in your own right. Yes, I would like to talk with Stephen after awhile; he had some very fine things to say.

Joan: Well, I'll say this: it was a great experience to receive Betty. Some very interesting things happened. There was the evening, for example, when Betty showed me how to speak through myself. I was a spirit speaking through my own mouth! Too many people forget that this sort of thing is possible; they don't contact their own spirits enough. I mean their *own* spirits—not their spirit friends.

Leichtman: We were experimenting with that a few nights ago.

Joan: Do you want to talk to David?

Leichtman: Well, not now, but maybe we ought to explain what you're talking about.

Joan: Well, a medium can engage his mediumship without necessarily entertaining a spook. It can be his own higher self which comes through the "trapdoor." This can be a rather complicated connection to make, but it can be quite worthwhile, especially for creative work. I believe someone plans to discuss this later on this evening.

Leichtman: Oh, good. Would you care to comment on the evolution of your own psychic awareness, as described in *Our Unseen Guest?* I personally thought it was a very fine record of someone slowly and meticulously developing, with the necessary doubt, to perfect her own skill.

Joan: Well, any intelligent person who found himself developing this skill would, I think, want to take the trouble to train it very carefully, with a proper amount of skepticism. After all, he's going to have to live with these abilities, and they are going to influence every other part of his life. I know that what I learned about myself along the way was, for me, by far the most important thing that came out of my development.

You know, of course, that Joan is not my real name, but we are going to have to use it, because that is the only name your readers are familiar with. I was relatively well known then in my own right in a business, and I just didn't want to compromise it. But people are going to have to speak out a bit more than they do.

Leichtman: It's safer to do so nowadays.

Joan: But the right people don't speak out.

Leichtman: I understand.

Joan: And they don't say what they think; they make all sorts of evasions and use artificial names. Of course, in my day an artificial name was almost necessary for other reasons. But it's time for people who do have values to speak about them, and not remain silent because they are in the minority. Most people nowadays seem to think that values are old fashioned but they are very important.

To go back to what I was saying, when you discover mediumistic or psychic skills growing within yourself, you should value yourself enough to want to train those skills properly, even if you are not comfortable with them in the beginning. As you know, I was not comfortable with mine at the beginning, and David went through a period of hesitation, too. It is always something to examine closely under the microscope of your mind—and even worry about—because everyone hears about the "Madame Zenobias" of the world, who keep giving readings long after their psychic abilities stop.

No matter what you do, if you're going to do a good job of it, you have to stop every once in awhile and question how things are going. Now, that's especially true of mediumship and psychic work! So many people seem to think, however, that you can just pop into trance—that you can decide to be a medium on Thursday and hold seances on Friday. Even if you have the skill, it doesn't work that way, because you need time to develop. You have to give yourself time to ask the proper questions about what's happening.

Winters: What kind of questions?

Joan: Whether what is coming out of your mouth is your own subconscious, your own feelings, your own opinions—or something from beyond. And, if it is coming from beyond, is it important enough to warrant listening to it? Certainly, many of the people who hold forth in seances have nothing important to say—and I'm talking about the invisibles, too. It's always good to keep in mind the time-honored saying: just because someone has "passed over," does not automatically mean that person is wise.

Leichtman: We've seen some good examples of that in public services at the local Spiritualist Church. It was authentic spiritism and mediumship, but it wasn't worth listening to.

Joan: It was authentic spiritism, but not authentic mediumship. There is a difference, you know.

Leichtman: There is?

Joan: Spiritism is the slavering and lusting after the voice of a spirit at the cost of everything else. I went to a number of Spiritualists, and frankly, I was disgusted at the obscene obsession for the voices of spirit. It really is obscene when that is all you are listening for.

Leichtman: And sacrilegious, too.

Joan: Certainly! And no way to honor Aunt Tillie, or whoever the spirit is. It's stupid! Why would you want to listen to a conversation which made no sense to anyone in the room?

Leichtman: What do you think about the current vogue of assuming that psychic and mediumistic abilities are best attained through utter passiveness and making the mind blank—so that a spirit or inspiration can somehow slip through it?

Joan: Well, of course that's not how it works. Nothing of value is ever gained by just doing nothing. I suppose someone has already mentioned this—one of the spooks over here is nodding his head that it has been covered—but I'm going to state it again. An intelligent person who discovers that he or she is psychic will want to know *why* and how to do it *better* and how to improve the *quality*. And in the course of answering those questions, he will learn a great deal about himself and how his subconscious works.

Anyway, I would be suspicious of anyone who actually succeeds in making his mind blank. Isn't that the state of catatonia?

Leichtman: Well, it's certainly mental deadness.

Joan: Well, it's not healthy.

Leichtman: No. You would wonder, "If he can really empty his mind and make it blank, was there all that much there in the first place?" [*Laughter.*]

Joan: Exactly. Why would someone want to stop his mind? I don't understand it. The mind is the chief organ we have for appreciating and knowing God. If we can't do that in some real sense, then life is a waste.

Leichtman: Yes, the mind is our organ for awareness in the earth plane.

Joan: If a medium makes his mind blank in order to go into trance, I will guarantee you that the blanks that come out of his mouth during the trance will be completely worthless. [*Laughter.*] Even Edgar Cayce—who is greatly misunderstood on this subject—would tell you that to go into trance your mind has to be the most acute, the most active, and the most aware and alert, because you are dying for a few minutes, every time you do it. You don't want to die permanently, but you want to allow a dear friend who hasn't had a mouth for some time to have a chance to speak again. Why in the world would you ever want to make your mind blank? You have to be the most alert then that you ever are in your whole life.

This is true of meditation, too—that's the time to be the most alert you possibly can. Any awareness that comes down from—dare I say "on high" without being misunderstood?—requires a great deal of alertness to catch. It is so light and tiny, if I may put it that way. It's very subtle. It's the famous "still, small voice within." And you have to be very alert to catch it.

The mind works like Grand Central Station used to be. It is terribly noisy, not in an unpleasant way, but because it's busy. And the person in meditation or the medium is listening for his child's voice way across this big, crowded, hectic room. And you do hear him, but it's through *attunement*, not blankness.

Think of it this way: God is certainly not a blank, and if we are all here to honor God, how can we do that by making ourself a blank? I think that the people who advocate blankness are probably the real Satanists—they are involved in a deadly sin. Being a nothing, a naught, a no-thing is a very, very great sin.

Leichtman: But many people encourage this as a way of being spiritual. They claim you have to start by "getting yourself out of the way."

Joan: What Satanist church do they belong to? [*Laughter.*]

Leichtman: Wow!

Joan: Well, that's what Satan is—the one who teaches people to be nothing, to be no-thing, a naught, a zero, a vegetable. Now, a real turnip is a beautiful thing, but a human who is trying to be a turnip is something gross. The whole proposition is repugnant.

David can tell you that just because I am talking at the moment does not mean that he is a nothing. He is hard at work at the moment. I won't tell you what he's doing, because it is none of your business, but he is very alert and aware.

Leichtman: May I ask some questions about how you viewed the material that came through you psychically? How important was the so-called "evidential material" for you, and how did you evaluate what was important and what was not?

Joan: Evidential material is always important. It is especially reassuring to have material come through that you can check on and find if it is really accurate.

The contents of *Our Unseen Guest* represent about a third of the material that we gathered. After it was published, of course, we got more. We were given a great deal of material which was personal, private, and conversational which would not have mattered to anyone else. The material we included in the book was chosen because we decided it was important to others. We also selected material on the basis that it was something new for us, and probably for others, too. Bear in mind that we could not go to a corner bookstore and buy all the books on these subjects you can now. In those days, books on the occult and psychic phenomena were very rare and hard to come by. Darby and I did not at that time live in California; it was easier for Betty and Stewart to buy books than for us at any time. So, out of all the material we had—and we had a mountain of it—we selected what we thought was important to the world.

Leichtman: I find this very interesting. You could have given all sorts of evidential material on the details of Stephen's incarnation, I suppose, but you didn't. You focused on other things.

Joan: We thought the other things were more important, and Stephen preferred that we not print some of the information he gave about himself. Incidentally, we did some limited checking on his incarnation, and we did find that what he was saying was the actual truth.

There is a parallel in the book *The Search for Bridey Murphy*, which is very full of evidentials. But how many times are you going to read it? Once is sufficient to get that book's basic message. It's an important book, but not the type you would read over and over again in order to absorb its content.

Leichtman: Ultimately, I suppose, it's not who did

what that is important, but the value and sense of the ideas presented.

Joan: And what the people involved learned along the way.

Leichtman: Yes. Stephen could have described an endless string of incarnations, but what he said instead was apparently quite worthwhile, and certainly helped you and Darby. It made sense.

Joan: I have to make a confession. Colene?

Colene Johnson: Yes?

Joan: Darby and I have been chuckling about how similiar the relationship between you and David is to what our's was like. We always felt the psychic things we did greatly enriched our relationship. I wanted to say this because psychic and mediumistic talents ought to make your life happier and fuller and richer. Do you know what I mean? Our love for each other was magnified ten times by every psychic step we took. And people need to know this—it is a gauge of whether they are doing it right or not. The best measure of your psychic development or spiritual growth is how it changes *the quality of your life*—what you learn from it and the joy you gain. In fact, that's the best measure of how well you are doing anything, psychic or not—the joy you derive from doing what you are supposed to be doing.

Leichtman: That brings to mind the many so-called mediums who grunt and groan and huff and puff about how "hard" they have to work to do their thing.

Joan: I don't see why it should be a strain.

Leichtman: They claim it is.

Joan: My goodness. David sometimes loses a little weight, but he can stand that once in awhile. I went through that, too. What's so terrible about that? Digging ditches or any type of work ought to do that.

I think we are going to change partners, if you don't mind.

Leichtman: Okay.

Joan: Thank you.

Leichtman: Thank you for coming.

[*Joan then withdrew from David's body and was replaced by Stephen.*]

Stephen: I suppose this is going to be a polyglot sort of seance. Stephen is the name I will have to use, but it's not the one I have been currently using. Most of you in the room know me by another name, but I won't fill you in on that. So, can we proceed from here?

Leichtman: All right. Let me pose a question to you that I addressed to Joan. In *Our Unseen Guest* you stressed the content and quality of what was said as being more important than minor trivial details about your previous physical existence.

Stephen: Well, isn't the content of a conversation far more important than the trivial details? Trivial personal details are all right in their place. Details about someone's recent incarnation are, I suppose, interesting at the moment. But if someone has something to say that's important, that is what should be listened to. My God, what if the Bible were only concerned with Jesus's private life? It would not be a living book. As a matter of fact, in today's modern society, it might even be considered X-rated. [*Laughter.*] Well, He was alive and well and healthy in the physical plane at one time. Otherwise, He wouldn't have been important. He had to have a physical life in

STEPHEN
In A Festive Mood

order to transcend it, didn't He?

I hope that answers you, Doctor?

Leichtman: Oh, yes. So often psychics and mediums waste their talents on people who demand enormous amounts of evidential details—to prove the validity of the skill—before they will listen to anything more significant.

Stephen: Yes.

Leichtman: And it's an appalling waste.

Stephen: One is certainly entitled to some kind of reassurance that what is coming through is accurate, but when that is all that is looked for, then something very important is missing. Let me suggest this: if you would think about the teachers you've had in this lifetime who've been very important to you, you would list those people who had something to say besides small talk. Small talk is very pleasant—it is one of life's minor joys, but it certainly is not the "end all" of life. Or the "be all," or whatever that cliche is. It escapes me at the moment. But my goodness, think how boring it would be only to talk about the weather forever and ever.

Leichtman: Can I ask what you are doing now?

Stephen: Well, at the moment I am sitting here tickling David. [*Laughter.*]

You know me quite well, but under a different name. We have had several conversations. And Colene knows me quite well, too. I think David has already figured out who I am. But I am very busy—with Rosie [one of David's spirit friends] I might add—helping a number of highly intelligent young people develop their mediumship, because it's going to be needed in the world. [*Shifting in the chair*] Handling a body after you've been out of one for awhile is sometimes a surprise.

Leichtman: Did you enjoy dinner?

Stephen: Oh, we all did. It was not the taste of the food, although I am sure the taste of the food was superior, Paul. [The meal had been prepared by Paul Winters.] Rather, it was the enjoyment of the group enjoying the food, which I suppose is what makes a dinner party even when you are in the physical, isn't it.

Leichtman: In terms of helping people develop their mediumship, are you preparing a few mediums who will be active in the scientific world and the political world, as well as the—

Stephen: Oh, yes.

Leichtman: And the educational world?

Stephen: And the arts, of course. There is a whole group of us working on this. There are about four hundred beings we are helping in whatever capacity we can. In several instances, they are under the age of five and, I am happy to say, are in family situations where they can become good mediums very early in life with no onus, no problem. They have families who love them and will do anything to help them do whatever they want to do.

Leichtman: I am intrigued. If one were an artist and a medium, how would he express his mediumship in the world of art?

Stephen: By painting, drawing, or sculpting.

Leichtman: I see. Would he go into a trance and someone would draw "through" him?

Stephen: Oh, no—of course not! He would enlist the aid of—oh, a Rembrandt, El Greco, or Goya—but these beings would act as a teacher. They would not take over the paintbrush and paint *for* the artist. They would teach.

Leichtman: All right.

Stephen: After all, one of the highest forms of clairvoyance known to man through all the centuries has been the inspiration of the fine arts. Even though most artists don't think of it in this way, it is a grounding of clairvoyance. Who cares what they think—that's the way it is!

Leichtman: How would a chemist or physicist apply his mediumship?

Stephen: By chemming and physing. [*Guffawing*].

Leichtman: What I'm getting at is—

Stephen: Those are proper English words. I'm sorry, but they are.

Leichtman: They sound like an Alka-Seltzer tablet. [*Laughter.*]

Stephen: You're spelling it wrong. The original gerund of the word "chemistry" is "chemming." The words "chemistry" and "alchemy" come from the real name of an ancient land that is known in modern times by the name of Egypt. It was originally known as *Khēmíā*. And the Egyptians were very good herbalists and chemists. Some of the great secrets of the ancient Egyptians involved their knowledge of chemical matters. These secrets were preserved to some degree in alchemy, which means "the study of the ancient lore of the Egyptians." The alchemists discovered some secrets about the chemical structure of things, and those discoveries gave rise to the modern science of chemistry. So, if you are a chemist working in your lab, you are chemming! And if you are a physicist doing your work, you are physing! [*Laughter.*]

I know that sounds funny, but I am serious. These are English words in good standing.

Leichtman: Well, how would a mediumistic physicist phys mediumistically? [*Laughter.*]

Stephen: I don't really understand physics, Doctor. I suppose he would split the atom in such a way that the astral body of the atom didn't become schizophrenic. [*Laughter.*]

Leichtman: But he wouldn't drop into a trance in order to run his experiments, would he?

Stephen: Oh, no.

Leichtman: Then the type of mediumship you're speaking of does not involve dead trance work in front of a group.

Stephen: Oh, God no! At times, trance work for groups can be helpful; great books do get written this way. But the mediumistic artist, musician, chemist, or physicist would "plug in" automatically while he was in the midst of working on his art, music, chemistry, or physics. There would be a shift in consciousness in which the object of his work became alive in a new and meaningful way.

Leichtman: I remember a very wise and gifted psychologist who said that as he wrote his books, his ideas "came" to him and told him how to write them down. I suppose that an invention or discovery could come to a physicist and tell him how to get itself invented or discovered.

Stephen: Or a painting could come to an artist to get painted, or a piece of music could come to a musician to be composed. And that is actually how it often happens, you know.

Hewitt: Are you saying, then, that these are

not original works of art?

Stephen: I am saying anything *but* that! They are original works, but the germ of them comes to the artist or musician or physicist in order to be drawn, composed, or discovered.

Hewitt: Yet the impetus is—

Stephen: They are original! I am not in any way decrying the artist's originality. You must shake out of your head any ideas you have about mediumship being passive. This kind of creative mediumship is anything but. It involves great originality and skill.

What I am describing is how an idea works itself out from the inner planes. It is an act of mediumship. The creative artist or musician or physicist must be impregnated with an idea. That idea already exists in a very abstract form, but for it to be created physically, it must be born in the mind and works of a creative human. And so it seeks one out.

It would be wrong to believe that the idea that then forms in the mind of the creative person, as a result of his mediumship, is not original. It is truly *his* idea, because he has shaped it with his skill, his abilities, and his knowledge. And it would also be wrong to think that the final painting, piece of music, or discovery was not his. He deserves the credit, because he has poured his time, his labors, and his love into the hard, arduous work of perfecting the physical form.

Leichtman: You seem to suggest that spirits sometimes serve as midwives for artistic creations.

Stephen: Oh, yes—but they are midwives, not the mothers. But this is why artistic and scientific creations are called brain children—because the throes of labor involved in creativity are just as severe and as painful as the throes of a mother having a baby.

Leichtman: The spooks always seem to have to use forceps in delivering my brain children. [*Laughter.*]

Stephen: I could make some X-rated comments, but I will refrain. [*More laughter.*]

Leichtman: The labor is terrible, I can tell you!

Stephen: Aww.

Leichtman: I say that for your benefit.

Stephen: John, if you would assume that an original idea is a fragment of God impregnating the mind of a human being, and then the human has to give birth to the idea, you may be better able to understand what I'm getting at.

Leichtman: Would that be a "virgin birth"? [*Laughter.*]

Hewitt: I was thinking of Mozart, who was writing full symphonies at the age of seven or eight. How could a child that age consciously construct those symphonies? The ability to do that must have come from beyond his conscious apparatus, and in a situation like that, it couldn't be an original effort on his part. The child must have been a channel for higher entities, who funneled these creations through him.

Stephen: I see what you mean, but don't forget that Mozart's own spirit would have been involved, too, and even a child can draw on talents learned in previous lives. No, it's still proper to give Mozart the full credit for originality.

At the same time, it is important to understand that human beings are *meant* to be channels of creativity—channels between the inner planes and the outer planes. That is why people are here, and it does not detract from their originality. Did you ever think about that?

Hewitt: Certainly.

Stephen: Whether it's just your ordinary, day-to-day life, or a creative project, you can make it a channel for something divine.

Leichtman: Would you say that, in a way, we are all mediums of our own spirit?

Stephen: I would say you all *should* be mediums for your own spirit, but very few are. That's not addressed to the people here in the room—it's addressed to whoever reads the book. And if you are doing it right, you also ought to be mediums for the Divine Spark.

And just because we begin to see that creative people are mediums in no way suggests that we should honor them less; we should honor them more. We should honor them for being an effective channel of creative inspiration, for developing creative skills, and for working hard to make it all happen. Mozart still had to have the basic musical skills, and even as a child he worked harder than most adults do all their lives. That deserves credit—and honor! And the same skills have to be developed by the people who do the chemming and physing.

Leichtman: Does an artist "art"? [*Laughter.*]

Stephen: Certainly, he "arts." Haven't you ever heard the expression, "Thou art"? So he picked up his paint brush and he did! [*More laughter.*]

Leichtman: I like that!

Stephen: Has this been talked about at all—that human laughter is one of the happiest things to hear in heaven?

Leichtman: Madame Blavatsky talked about it.

Stephen: Oh, I'm glad she did, because she was probably more eloquent on the subject than I could be. Enjoying laughter is just the grandest thing. We enjoy it even more on the inner planes than you do on the outer planes. It's our champagne, you know.

Leichtman: Well, I don't want to break this mood, but since you equated creativity with childbirth, I'd like to ask also about the creative equivalent of abortion. I'm talking about ideas and inspirations that are not earthed or manifested. Are the implications as severe as with a physical abortion?

Stephen: It's not really an abortion. In a physical abortion, you remove something. In what you just called a creative abortion, however, nothing is removed.

If a creative idea is not grounded in one lifetime, it will be grounded in the next—or the next or the next or the one after that. But the inflammation of that "dead fetus of the mind" does create mental and emotional problems in the personality. To be healthy, a creative person does have to give birth to his creative ideas. And it really is giving birth.

Leichtman: I presume that while there is not any dead tissue to be removed or reabsorbed—

Stephen: There are dead ideas. Well, they are not really dead—they are encysted.

Leichtman: And it is energy that is not focused but it remains there—

Stephen: So it falls under the laws of karma, doesn't it? You are supposed to do something which you do not do, and so there is going to be a karmic reaction to the lack of action. Karma is the principle of action/reaction. Eventually, the cyst will open and be born again, but maybe not in this lifetime. And so, if you block the birth channel of your creative ideas, you are going to have to suffer the "inflammation" that results.

Leichtman: As a corollary to that, I have found that in dealing with people who are frustrated in their domestic life or their work, the pursuit of a creative hobby will help get the energy flowing again from the inner levels to the outer. It can unblock a variety of positive qualities and energies, even though their artistic creations may never please anyone except themselves.

Stephen: Of course. You should always give birth to whatever ideas inspire you. You wouldn't always want to put them out for society to view, but the birthing is very important.

Leichtman: As Betty and Stewart talked about an "awareness mechanism" in their books, is there also a creative or a creativity mechanism?

Stephen: Oh, yes.

Leichtman: And would this creativity mechanism be something which can be focused in any aspect of your life?

Stephen: Absolutely. The creativity mechanism is a part of the awareness mechanism. It is, in fact, the healthy grounding of the awareness mechanism. I am talking about creativity of all different kinds now—even including the preparation of the spaghetti this evening.

Leichtman: I suppose this is part of what Cayce meant when he used to admonish people to use what they have.

Stephen: That is a profoundly important idea.

Using what you have is the best way to obtain more.

Leichtman: Lusting after it doesn't work?

Stephen: No. There's been a lot of talk today about developing psychic and mediumistic talents, but still most people do prefer to lust after those talents, rather than use what they have productively. Yet using what they have is what opens room for more to develop. Let me explain it this way: if you get a creative idea and then write it down, or draw it, or put it in a piece of music, then you've made room for the next good idea, haven't you?

Leichtman: Yes. You've broken the logjam.

Stephen: Well, you've broken the bag of waters. [*Laughter.*] No, I intend to keep the idea in terms of pregnancy, because that's what it really is.

Winters: Earlier it was mentioned that people have been both sexes at various times in earlier lives. I wonder how some people would respond to that idea—especially someone not well versed in occultism.

Leichtman: It offends their sexual chauvinism. An enlightened human being must have both the male and female principles of consciousness operative, because everyone must be able to get out and *do* things—and that's an expression of the male principle—and everyone must be able to be loving, gentle, and kind—and that's a manifestation of the female principle.

It has nothing to do with the physical "plumbing."

Stephen: It never did.

Leichtman: While we are on this, there is a myth floating around that's been promoted by dilettante reincarnationists—

Stephen: I wonder what the gerund of *that* is.

Leichtman: I wouldn't try it.

Stephen: Isting? [*Laughter.*] Or carning? [*More laughter.*] I think what you are talking about is carning—which is an English word meaning "being a member of a carnival." [*Giggling.*]

Leichtman: Oh, really!

Stephen: Of course, I forgot that you don't speak English.

Leichtman [*facetiously*]: Being a native of Saturn, that's right.

Stephen: No, you speak "American," which is a different language.

Leichtman: Anyway, would you comment on the myth that homosexuality is due to an abrupt change of sex from the last incarnation to the current one?

Stephen: When you stop and think about all the millions of people that are and will be and have been, giving *one* reason for anything is ridiculous. There are as many reasons for being heterosexual as there are heterosexual people. There are as many reasons for being homosexual as there are homosexual people. And nobody decides an issue like that on the level of the personality. The necessary lessons to be learned in any one lifetime are part of the life mission, and that's selected before birth.

I am not making moral statements condoning or forgiving anything now; I'm just describing what happens. One is a man or a woman because that experience is necessary at that particular time. One is a Chinese or a Negro or a white because that experience is necessary at that particular time. But the decisions of what is necessary and when are made individually—not in terms of everybody. And anyone who sets forth a generalization—such as "all people who have blue eyes are Atlantean incarnations"—is just being silly.

Leichtman [facetiously]: Of course—Atlanteans had brown eyes. [*Laughter.*]

Stephen: Think of how many people are born in China who are reincarnations of Atlanteans. They have no hope of having a blue eye—much less two.

Leichtman: That's another occult "truism" that is frequently tossed around: "Now, at last, the Atlanteans are starting to come back into incarnation"—apparently after having to wait thousands of years.

Stephen: I'm going to be quite blunt. The people who say such things are demonstrating their complete lack of imagination. A small child with an active imagination could come up with a better story than that. The economy of the universe would not allow someone to lounge around heaven for thousands or millions of years. The Atlanteans never stopped reincarnating. The Lemurians never stopped reincarnating. It's an absurdity.

Leichtman: In the life readings I've done, I've never found anyone who did not have an Atlantean incarnation—and plenty in between.

Stephen: My friend Dr. Kammutt [an inner planes teacher] has said this, but I am going to restate it for the record: everyone of you has lived ten thousand times ten thousand lifetimes in the physical plane. And you will probably live that many more. Those who go around playing the reincarnation game, saying that they *know* this is going to be their last incarnation and that they have completed their evolution, are very foolish. If you thought about it for three minutes, you would know these people can't possibly be off the wheel of rebirth—if they were, they would be Bodhisattvas and they'd willingly come back to help all the rest of humanity.

Leichtman: Yes, it's when you don't *have to* reincarnate—

Stephen: That you especially want to.

Leichtman: Because that's when you can help the most.

Stephen: The idiotic teaching that the physical plane is a kind of purgatory or punishment has created a lot of these ideas, you know. When the idea of reincarnation was reintroduced into the West, people began to believe that reincarnation is a punishment. It's nothing of the kind. Well, I suppose it is for *some* people, but they are the ones who made it that way. They determined the difficulties they may be facing, by their own actions and attitudes.

You know, the only recording angel you are answerable to is your own inner spirit. He's the one who really keeps the books; it's he that knows when you've been bad and good—not Santa Claus. [*Laughter.*] When you pass over, you do confront your own spirit, but why would anyone be afraid of confronting his own spirit? And why would anyone be afraid of the future? It has been determined by your own spirit—and by your own actions, thoughts, and feelings.

And anyway, what's wrong with life? What's so terrible about living?

Leichtman: Nothing that I know of. There's a famous quotation from Edgar Cayce that refers to Atlanteans reincarnating in greater abundance nowadays. Does that have to do with the fact that some of the people who once focused great ability in art or science or literature can now begin to express their skills again, because our civilization and technology is once more coming up to the levels of their genius?

Stephen: Do I get equal air time? [*Laughter.*]

Leichtman: Well, I want to be fair to Edgar.

Stephen: To be really fair to Edgar, it must be realized that Edgar's work has suffered by editing. What Edgar really said and what the books say Edgar said do not always coincide.

Edgar was talking about a group of people who are incarnating rather quickly at the present time, and they were Atlanteans—but so was almost everyone else who is on the face of the earth at the moment. Bear in mind that Atlantis was a very long-lived culture and civilization and a great number of people incarnated during that period. Many people incarnated a great many times *during* the Atlantean epoch. Everybody in this room had Atlantean lifetimes, myself included. Edgar was referring to a specific group of people who will be born over and over again rather quickly here at the beginning of the Aquarian Age.

[*Joking*] And no, you are not in limbo, Paul. Limbo can't possibly happen. The Aquarian Age began in 1968, as it was announced at that time by the White Brotherhood. I thought I would clear the record on these points for you—you are too young for gray hair. [*Laughter.*]

I do enjoy my jokes—I give lessons to Rosie [Rosie, one of David's invisible friends, has a very light sense of humor].

Leichtman: Oh, really?

Stephen: And she gives lessons to me.

Leichtman: Good. Now, before we finish, I want you to comment on a subject I know you're an expert on: "the rape of the mind" or the rape of the "metaphysical bride."

Stephen: Well, I think the best way to comment on that is to keep the image I used earlier going—the idea of creativity as a form of pregnancy.

Leichtman: We don't want this book X-rated.

Stephen: No, we can talk about this in perfectly dignified terms.

Leichtman: Oh, thank goodness! [*Laughter.*]

Stephen: This is what happens: many people suddenly feel a creative urge and they go flying to their paintbrushes or typewriters, only to turn out something horrible and disgusting, because they have been mentally raped into accepting a mediocre value system. Now, that is one of the worst forms of rape going—that someone will not have faith in his own value system, but accepts someone else's. "Keeping up with the Joneses" is a variety of this—the urge to keep up appearances. The awful thing is that no one else is raping these people—they are raping themselves, over and over. Almost every thought that comes out of their mind, after the initial rape, is going to be stillborn. It's most unfortunate.

I have to put it in these terms, Doctor—it has to be stated dramatically, because it's a very serious problem! Accepting someone else's values for your life is the greatest mistake anyone can make. The only being you should take your values from is God. And after you've listened to God, you should evaluate it for yourself, because that's part of the creative process of living. But you are denying your own humanity if you accept someone else's value system as your own. That's against God! It's Satanism.

There's a directive given by Jesus in the Bible to look for Him in every person. And the first one you should look for Him in is yourself, in your values. Look first to your own values, then look for and honor those same values in others. And once you find your values within you, then learn to live by them.

You should find great joy in discovering the Christ consciousness within. Then you can take that joy and look for it in every other man and woman. Should they not know about it themselves, you should then quietly and humbly help them find it, too.

The rape of the "metaphysical bride" is somewhat different. The metaphysical bride is the subconscious mind and the inner workings of the mind below the logical level. Both men and women have this metaphysical bride; it has nothing to do with one's sex.

Now, you need to treat the metaphysical bride like an honored wife. It is the mother, after all, of your brain children. You should even celebrate your golden wedding anniversary with your metaphysical bride, because you were actually married a long, long time ago. [*Laughter.*] But unfortunately, most people do not honor the bride; they rape it over and over again, by the way they pile garbage into their subconsciouses.

The metaphysical bride is vastly important to anyone developing his spiritual awareness, his occult ability, his mediumship, or his creativity, because it is the metaphysical bride that opens the door to these capacities. But if you have raped the bride, by dumping into your subconscious all the garbage of your thoughts, passions, habits, animosities, and twisted feelings, when she opens the door to psychic ability or creativity, the inspiration that comes in is going to collect some of this garbage. The metaphysical bride can't help it; she doesn't want it, but there you have it. You have raped her and left her with it.

Now, if you prize her, honor her, and treat her properly, then when you open the door to your genius or your psychic awareness, something clean will come in and she will greet it like the hostess of your house would. She will keep your mental household clean and in order and do all sorts of wonderful things to support your daily activities. But I'm not going to go into any more detail, because it would be a mistake here.

Leichtman: What about people who treat their subconscious as though they were Nazi stormtroopers goosestepping through Europe? I'm referring to those people who shout militant self-hypnotic commands and affirmations at their subconscious.

Stephen: Would a kind and loving husband goosestep over his wife and shout commands? I know what male chauvinism is—it's just as stupid as female chauvinism. But the kind of chauvinistic attitude which encourages people to stomp on their own minds is—and again I'm sorry to have to say this—another kind of Satanism.

There's an old saying that I will close with: the devil is stupidity. He's not stupid—*he is stupidity!* The idea of stomping on your own mind, of trying to be a no-thing, of being militantly stupid, of accepting someone else's values—these ideas are the devil. The devil isn't some satanic entity sitting somewhere in hell—the Satan most people have to worry about is the one they have let develop within themselves.

And that is something which should be meditated on by everyone in the room—and everyone who will read this.

And with that, I am going to leave you.

Leichtman: Thank you for coming.

GLOSSARY

ALCHEMY: The art of transmuting substances into more precious materials. As applied to the physical plane, alchemy is the precursor of modern chemistry. In its more esoteric application, however, alchemy is a practical system of magic and a symbol of the transmutation of the impurities of the personality under the guidance of the soul.

ALPHA BODY: A term coined by the Whites to refer to the physical form of any unit of consciousness. The alpha body of a human being would be the physical body.

ANGEL: An entity belonging to the angelic or devic kingdom. Angels are not discarnate humans and have never been humans—they are part of a separate kingdom of life, and have their own function and evolution. Still, their work and interests do bring them in touch with humans quite frequently—although humans are often unaware of this contact, as angels are invisible to ordinary sight. The angelic kingdom includes natures spirits, angels, and archangels.

AQUARIAN AGE: The coming epoch in civilization. It will last approximately 2,000 years and be marked by an increasing awareness in humanity of the value of brotherhood and service.

ASTRAL BODY: Any vehicle of life made of astral matter; in humans, the body of the emotions.

ASTRAL PLANE: The plane of the emotions and desires. The astral plane is an inner world made of matter that is more subtle than physical substance, and yet it interpenetrates all physical substance. It is teeming with life of its own.

ASTRAL TRAVEL: Any form of movement of an entity on the astral plane. Simply expressing a strong emotion can be a form of astral travel. Often, this term is used to describe the psychic phenomenon of separating the astral body from the physical body and projecting it to a distant location. Astral travel is called "soul travel" by some, but that is a misnomer. The soul pervades everything; it does not have to travel.

ATLANTEAN: A long stage in human development and civilization when the primary focus of human growth was the nurturing and expression of the astral body or emotions. This period is named "Atlantis" because it was primarily centered on a now-submerged continent in the Atlantic Ocean and was referred to by this name by Plato in his accounts of it. The heyday of Atlantean culture was from approximately 100,000 to 12,000 B.C., but included many different stages.

AURA: The light observed by clairvoyants around all life forms. It emanates from the surface and interior of the etheric, astral, and mental bodies. Clairvoyant observation of the aura can give an indication of the quality of health or consciousness in the individual.

AWARENESS MECHANISM: A term coined by the Whites to describe the equipment of consciousness used to perceive phenomena.

BETA BODY: A term coined by the Whites to refer to "the form attribute of that frequency which is an individual consciousness." The term is synonymous with "mental body."

BODHISATTVA: A Sanskrit word signifying the full enlightenment of substance. In other words, a Bodhisattva is an individual who has raised the quality of his personality—his mind, emotions, and physical body—to such a degree that they are a perfect expression of his higher, divine nature. As a result, he has succeeded in the task of bringing heaven to earth; the life of the Bodhisattva is the demonstration that the spiritual goal of life is *not* to escape the world and its limitations, but rather to conquer those limitations and achieve illumination through full and active service in rendering the physical plane more enlightened.

BUDDHIC PLANE: The plane of spiritual intuition. The buddhic plane, so named because it embodies the principle of "buddhi" or "realization," is an inner world or plane of existence that is more subtle than the physical, astral, or mental planes, yet interpenetrates the substance of those planes. It teems with life and purpose of its own. A human being must be able to focus in the light of his soul in order to operate consciously on the buddhic plane, as the human personality is not equipped with senses able to perceive the subtle substance of the buddhic.

CAUSAL BODY: The form aspect of the soul, so named because it exists at the level of causes—the abstract levels of the mental plane. Whereas the human personality is reconstructed at the beginning of each incarnation, the causal body remains constant throughout the long series of incarnations of any soul. In many ways, the causal body *is* the soul, and yet it is really only the form of the soul, not the consciousness of the soul.

CLAIRVOYANCE: The capacity to see or know beyond the limits of the physical senses. There are many degrees of clairvoyance, allowing the clairvoyant to comprehend forces, beings, and objects of the inner worlds normally invisible to the average person.

CO-EXISTENT ESSENCE: A term coined by the Whites to refer to the manifestations of consciousness at dense or "obstructed" levels. In the human being, the co-existent essence would be the personality; on a macrocosmic level, it would be time, space, and motion.

CONSCIOUSNESS: The capacity to know and be aware. It must be distinguished from *sensation,* which is the perception of objects, feelings, conditions, events, or ideas through the five physical senses or their emotional and mental counterparts. *Consciousness* is the ability of a unit of intelligence to reason on, reflect about, and draw conclusions regarding the nature of any other unit of intelligence or its manifestation—including itself. Descartes' statement, "I think, therefore I am," captures the spirit of consciousness. Esoterically, consciousness is the mechanism used by the soul to perceive life and interact with it, whereas sensation is the mechanism used by the personality—until it is able to work with consciousness.

ENLIGHTENMENT: Focused in the light of the soul. An enlightened mind is one that is capable of directly contacting the soul and using its light to perceive, comprehend, and apply the soul's wisdom. An enlightened personality is one that is governed and directed by an enlightened mind, in tune with the wisdom and love of the soul.

ETHERIC: Of, or pertaining to, the most subtle realm of the dense physical plane. The etheric is composed of the finest grades of physical matter, exceeding even the "fineness" of gases.

EVOLUTION: The growth of any life form to its destined perfection. It is the response of consciousness to the divine impulse to grow.

FEMALE PRINCIPLE: The receptive side of consciousness. In the human, the female principle expresses itself through such elements as the intuition, the emotions, the enjoyment of beauty, worship, and the capacity to grow. In the world, it expresses itself through nature and instinct. Esoterically, it is embodied by the World Mother.

FOURTH DIMENSION: A realm of existence in which there can be four different planes of movement from a single point, each of those planes being separated by ninety degrees. All physical solids are part of this large, fourth-dimensional realm. The movement of a fourth-dimensional solid through the physical plane would be recognized as a change in the apparent three-dimensional shape of that object, such as in the growth of a tree. We act in fourth-dimensional ways every day—by associating relevant memories to current experience, by speculating about our future, and by perceiving underlying motives and attitudes of other people. Loosely speaking, the astral plane could be considered the fourth dimension.

INCARNATION: The period of time in which a human spirit is expressing itself through a personality.

INNER PLANES: A term used to refer to any one of several inner worlds or levels of existence, all of which interpenetrate the dense physical plane. Each physical human being exists on these inner planes as well as on the physical level, by dint of having bodies composed of matter drawn from them. Most human beings do not consciously use these inner bodies, however, which either operate subconsciously or are partially inactive—until activated by personal growth and the development of intuitive awareness.

INVISIBLE: In this book, a discarnate entity.

KARMA: A Sanskrit word meaning "reactiveness." Every one of our actions, thoughts, and emotions produces a reaction of like quality, sooner or later. Good deeds and thoughts produce beneficient reactions; cruel and selfish deeds and thoughts produce restrictive reactions. By dealing with these karmic effects, we gradually learn the lessons of maturity.

KEYBOARD: An analogy developed in this series, likening the subconscious of a medium to the keyboard of an organ. The spirit speaking through the medium does so by "playing the keys" or "pulling the stops," as appropriate, within the medium's subconscious.

KOAN: Paradoxical or nonsensical statements formulated by Zen masters to stimulate the reflection of their students. An example of a koan is "the sound of one hand clapping."

LEMURIAN: A name used to represent the stage

of human evolution which preceded the Atlantean civilization and focused primarily on the development of physical and etheric expression. A person with a "Lemurian consciousness" would be one who was primarily focused physically—for example, was more highly motivated by primordial instincts than by either emotional drives or mental ideals.

"MADAME ZENOBIA": A personal term used to describe the type of emotional and unintelligent people whose lust for psychic experience and attention far exceeds their competence or honesty. Their appearance is often notable because of the excess of makeup, jewelry, and oddness of clothing. Despite the obvious handicap, they presume great psychic talent and hold forth as "gifted" clairvoyants and fortune tellers.

MALE PRINCIPLE: The active and expansive side of consciousness. In the human, the male principle expresses itself through such elements as the intellect, the pursuit of discovery, leadership, and work. In the world, it manifests through the mineral kingdom, electricity, and fire. Esoterically, it is the spirit or Father.

MATERIALISM: The belief or attitude that the physical plane is the only plane of existence, or at least the most powerful and important. Materialism denies the central importance of the soul, the existence of universal intelligence, and the invisible realms of life. It is the basis of black magic and leads the person who believes in it to become "earthbound"—a state in which all values, decisions, and acts are formulated in selfish and temporal terms.

MATTER: The substance of life—energy in manifestation. There is mental and astral matter as well as physical matter.

MEDITATION: An act of mental rapport in which the ideals, purposes, and intents of the higher self are discerned, interpreted, and applied to the personality. To be meaningful, meditation must be a very active state in which creative ideas, new realizations, and inspirations are pursued with vigor.

MEDIUM: A person who practices mediumship by conscious choice.

MEDIUMSHIP: The phenomenon of a nonphysical intelligence, usually a discarnate human, assuming some degree of control of a physical body in order to communicate something useful and meaningful. Mediumship is usually used for the transmission of information and inspired guidance, but can also be used to transmit varieties of healing energies.

MENTAL BODY: A separate body or vehicle of intelligence possessed by every human and interpenetrating the dense physical body. In essence, it is the mind. The mental body is composed of matter drawn from the mental plane. It is used for intellectual discernment, analysis, and logical thinking.

MENTAL HOUSECLEANING: The process of organizing and disciplining the mind and its contents: thoughts, attitudes, convictions, habits, and feelings. This work is a necessary part of attaining and preserving mental health, just as physical housecleaning is a necessary part of keeping one's living quarters neat, clean, and livable. When mental housecleaning is ignored, conditions of psychological illness can occur. The goal of mental housecleaning is to put in order and cleanse one's subconscious associations, beliefs, and behavior patterns. This process is most effective when authority for it is given to the soul.

MENTAL PLANE: The dimension of intellectual thought. One of the inner planes of existence, it also interpenetrates the dense physical plane. It teems with active life of its own, in addition to providing the substance for the mental bodies of all humanity.

METAPHYSICAL BRIDE: The portion of the human subconscious that has the capacity to express the feminine principle in a spiritual manner.

OCCULT: The hidden secrets of nature. The study of the occult deals not just with the esoteric aspects of man's being, but also the entire universe. It includes the study of the function, operation, purpose, origin, and destiny of nature and man. The word "occult" literally means "that which is hidden."

ORTHIC: Pertaining to "orthos," a term coined by the Whites to refer to the unobstructed or pure operation of consciousness, apart from form.

PERSONALITY: That part of a human being that is used for manifestation in the earth plane. Composed of a mind, emotions, and a physical body, it is the child of the soul and its experience on earth.

PETER PAN DEPARTMENT: A personal term for the realms of fantasy on the astral plane. Because astral substance is easily manipulated, fantasies can be generated that have no basis in reality but nonetheless appear real. In the Peter Pan Department, the objects of fantasy, fiction, and hallucinations become animated; people who lack discrimination are often deceived into believing that these animated characters and objects are actually alive.

PRANA: A Sanskrit word that can be translated "pre-breath." Prana is the vital energy that animates all etheric forms, making physical life possible. There are many grades and functions of prana.

PSYCHIC: A person who is able to perceive events and information without the use of the physical senses. The word is also used to refer to any event associated with the phenomena of parapsychology.

SEANCE: The event of a discarnate spirit entity speaking through a medium, in order to communicate with physical people.

SPIRIT: In this book, a term used primarily to describe the portion of the human being that survives death. It is this "spirit" that a medium contacts. In this sense, a spirit would be as individualistic as his or her personality was during physical life, retaining both good and bad characteristics. The word is also used to refer to the highest immortal, divine essence within the human being.

SPIRITISM: Any use of mediumship or clairvoyance motivated only by the lust for contact with spirits.

SPIRITUAL BODY: A term coined by the Whites to refer to any nonphysical body. In most cases, it was used to describe the body of emotions (the astral body), which is the body of manifestation for most spirits. It is not a very precise term to use, as the astral body of most people is far from spiritual.

SPIRITUALISM: A religious movement that incorporates mediumship as a central feature of its worship service and investigation of spiritual values.

SUBCONSCIOUS: The part of the personality that is not being consciously used at any given moment. The subconscious is always active and greatly influences our conscious moods, thoughts, acts, and attitudes. It is physically in tune with other portions of the inner planes—even if we are not consciously psychic at all.

SUBTLE REALMS: The inner planes of existence, so named because all perceptions at these levels are a good deal more subtle than perceptions at the physical level.

SUPERCONSCIOUS: Those elements of awareness which transcend the consciousness of the personality. The superconscious would include the consciousness of the soul, as well as even more transcendent kinds of awareness—for example, planetary or solar consciousness.

TRANCE: A state in which ordinary consciousness is quieted so that another element of consciousness can use the physical voicebox and body. In a hypnotic trance, the subconscious assumes control of the body. In a mediumistic trance, another entity takes over.

TRAPDOOR: A special connection in consciousness which permits a spirit to enter the subconscious of a medium in trance. Only people with this trapdoor can be genuine mediums.

VAMPIRE: One who saps or steals energy from another individual telepathically or psychically.

VESTIBULE: Not a specific location, but rather an experience in adjustment to the conditions of the inner planes after the death of the physical body. In the vestibule, the individual may receive healing, be reunited with loved ones in the spirit, or be instructed in the nature of life on the inner planes. The time spent in the vestibule varies from one individual to the next.

WHITE BROTHERHOOD: One of a number of select groups whose members are dedicated to the advancement of human evolution and the fulfillment of cosmic plans. It is composed of both incarnate and discarnate individuals, but functions on the inner planes.

ZEN: A form of mysticism practiced in Japan. Although the principles of Zen are gaining some popularity in the United States, their passive nature tends to interfere with the development of the mind, rather than encourage it.

FROM HEAVEN TO EARTH

The complete series of 12 interviews is available by subscription for $27 (for overseas delivery, $30). Each interview is published as a paperback book such as this one.

The spirits interviewed are Edgar Cayce, William Shakespeare, Cheiro, Carl Jung and Sigmund Freud, C.W. Leadbeater, Sir Oliver Lodge, Thomas Jefferson, Arthur Ford, H.P. Blavatsky, Nikola Tesla, Eileen Garrett, and Stewart White. All 12 books are now in print.

Orders can be placed by sending a check for the proper amount to Ariel Press, 2557 Wickliffe Road, Columbus, Ohio 43221-1899. Please make checks payable, in U.S. funds, to Ariel Press, or charge to MasterCard, VISA, or American Express. Ohio residents should add 5½% sales tax.

Individual copies of the interviews are also available, at $3 plus $1 postage each, when ordered from the publisher. When 10 or more copies of a *single* title are ordered, the cost is $2 per book plus the actual cost of shipping.

These books may also be purchased through your favorite bookstore.

THE PRIESTS OF GOD

Due to the popularity of the first series of 12 books in *From Heaven to Earth,* a second series of 12 interviews is also being conducted by Dr. Robert R. Leichtman and is available by subscription.

The spirits interviewed in this second series are all individuals who demonstrated a remarkable capacity to act with genius, leadership, and inspiration in their respective fields. The 12 spirits are Albert Schweitzer, Rembrandt, Sir Winston Churchill, Paramahansa Yogananda, Mark Twain, Albert Einstein, Benjamin Franklin, Andrew Carnegie, Richard Wagner, Luther Burbank, and Abraham Lincoln. The final book will be an interview with a number of spirits, titled *The Destiny of America.* A new book is published every three months. The series will be completely in print by October 1983.

The cost of subscribing to all 12 books is $27, postpaid. Orders can be placed by sending a check for the proper amount to Ariel Press, 2557 Wickliffe Road, Columbus, Ohio 43221-1899. Make checks payable to Ariel Press. Foreign checks should be payable in U.S. funds. Orders can also be charged to MasterCard, VISA, or American Express. In Ohio, please add 5½% sales tax.

Individual copies of the interviews are available at $3 plus $1 postage each. If 10 or more copies of *a single title* are ordered at one time, the price is $2 a book plus the actual costs of shipping.

THE WAY TO HEALTH

How much do you control your personal health? Do you understand the origins of health—and know how to attain it?

A book from Ariel Press, *The Way To Health,* answers these questions. Its authors, Robert R. Leichtman, M.D. and Carl Japikse, go beyond the usual prescriptions and theories of medicine, holistic health, and metaphysics and lucidly set forth a system for building health on all levels—physically, emotionally, mentally, and spiritually. The contents deal with the origins of health, the secret of vitality, the diagnosis of our invisible anatomy, and the attainment of health.

The Way To Health is written to help both health professionals and the general public. It is based on Dr. Leichtman's vast experience as a specialist in internal medicine, holistic health, spiritual healing, and psychic diagnosis, and Mr. Japikse's work in teaching and healing. The two essays printed in *The Way To Health* were originally published as part of *The Art of Living* essay series.

The Way To Health sells for $3, plus $1 for postage. To order, send a check or money order (in U.S. funds) for the proper amount to Ariel Press, 2557 Wickliffe Road, Columbus, Ohio 43221-1899. In Ohio, please add 5½% sales tax.

The Way To Health may also be purchased through your favorite bookstore.